MILLER

THE
CRUCIBLE

NOTES

COLES EDITORIAL BOARD

Bound to stay open

Publisher's Note

Otabind (Ota-bind). This book has been bound using the patented Otabind process. You can open this book at any page, gently run your finger down the spine, and the pages will lie flat.

ABOUT COLES NOTES

COLES NOTES have been an indispensible aid to students on five continents since 1948.

COLES NOTES are available for a wide range of individual literary works. Clear, concise explanations and insights are provided along with interesting interpretations and evaluations.

Proper use of COLES NOTES will allow the student to pay greater attention to lectures and spend less time taking notes. This will result in a broader understanding of the work being studied and will free the student for increased participation in discussions.

COLES NOTES are an invaluable aid for review and exam preparation as well as an invitation to explore different interpretive paths.

COLES NOTES are written by experts in their fields. It should be noted that any literary judgement expressed herein is just that — the judgement of one school of thought. Interpretations that diverge from, or totally disagree with any criticism may be equally valid.

COLES NOTES are designed to supplement the text and are not intended as a substitute for reading the text itself. Use of the NOTES will serve not only to clarify the work being studied, but should enhance the reader's enjoyment of the topic.

ISBN 0-7740-3021-6

© COPYRIGHT 1994 AND PUBLISHED BY
COLES PUBLISHING COMPANY
TORONTO—CANADA
PRINTED IN CANADA

Manufactured by Webcom Limited
Cover finish: Webcom's Exclusive **Duracoat**

CONTENTS

Arthur Miller: Life and Works

Arthur Miller was born in the Harlem section of Manhattan on October 17, 1915, the second son of a well-to-do clothing manufacturer whose eldest son followed him into the business. Arthur's interests, however, were football, hockey and, as he says, ". . . just fooling around." In fact, he was 17 before he read anything more serious than the Rover Boy books.

The Millers moved to Brooklyn while Arthur was still a young boy. He graduated from high school there in 1932 with a poor scholastic record, which prevented him from being accepted at the University of Michigan. He went to work in an auto parts warehouse instead, but soon became convinced that he really wanted to continue his studies at college. Miller was finally admitted to the University of Michigan in 1934, after waging an intensive campaign to get the admissions department to reverse its original verdict.

At the university, Miller began to write plays almost at once. In his sophomore and junior years, he gained a certain amount of recognition by winning the Avery Hopwood Award for the best student play. He failed to win the prize in his senior year, but he subsequently submitted the drama to the Theatre Guild whose National Award was given to him in 1938, the year of his graduation. He shared the Theatre Guild award with a southern aspirant one year his senior: Tennessee Williams.

Immediately after leaving the university, Miller joined the W.P.A.-sponsored Federal Theatre Project, then in its last years. While working with this group, he wrote a tragedy about the conquest of Mexico, which has never been published or performed. Miller remained with the Project until it ended. He then returned to New York where he earned his living for a few years by writing radio scripts, which he found an uncongenial occupation because, as he later observed, in radio drama every emotion must have a label. It helped to pay the rent, however, and made it possible for him to marry a college classmate, Mary Agnes Slattery. They had two children before the marriage ended in divorce.

In 1941, Miller was rejected by the armed forces because of a high-school football injury. He kept busy during the war years by writing scripts for army training films, working in the Brooklyn Navy Yard and visiting army camps where he gathered material for his first book, *Situation Normal,* published in 1944. It was during this time, too, that he did research for *The Story of G. I. Joe,* a movie about the well-known correspondent, Ernie Pyle. In 1945, Miller published his second book, *Focus,* the subject of which was anti-Semitism. Critics regarded it as "eloquent" but "too pat."

Since then, Miller has devoted himself almost exclusively to the theater. His first produced play was *The Man Who Had All the Luck,* written in 1944 and presented on Broadway the following year. It closed a week later. This failure was succeeded by a triumph—*All My Sons*—in 1947. This study of a dishonest wartime airplane-parts manufacturer established Miller's reputation. It won the three top awards in the New York theater: The Drama Critics' Circle Award, the Antoinette Perry Award and the Donaldson Award. A year later, *Death of a Salesman* was produced on Broadway. It won all the awards that he had previously earned, plus a Pulitzer Prize.

During the McCarthy era of the 1950's, Miller, whose politics represented the liberal intellectual outlook, was questioned by the House Un-American Activities Committee. He was indicted for contempt of Congress after refusing to answer questions about the activities of his acquaintances. One result of this legal altercation was *The Crucible,* a historical drama based on the Salem witchcraft trials with an implied analogy to the activity of the McCarthy group. The terror inspired even in innocent people, in both cases, the "handing over of conscience" to an outside authority, seemed to Miller a parallel too striking to go unremarked. When it came to Broadway in 1953, *The Crucible* met a mixed public and critical reaction, inevitably colored by the political temper of its time. It has been revived several times in America and has also found a warm reception from European audiences.

Miller's next plays, *A View from the Bridge* and *A Memory of Two Mondays,* were produced as a double bill in 1955. *After the Fall,* which marked his return to the theater after an eight-year silence, opened at the Lincoln Center Repertory Theatre in 1963. This thinly disguised autobiographical work received generally favorable critical reviews, although some observers felt that Miller was too frank with details of his second marriage.

During Miller's second marriage, to Marilyn Monroe, his only literary output was a motion picture scenario, *The Misfits,* which he wrote for his wife in 1959. This movie was described by many critics as original and penetrating. Miller and Marilyn Monroe were subsequently divorced, and he then married a German photographer, Ingeborg Morath.

As a man of independent thought, Miller is profoundly and angrily concerned with what he perceives as the immediate issues of our society: the irresponsible pressures that are brought to bear upon free men, the self-seeking that blinds whole segments of our civilization to justice, the evasions and dishonesties into which cowardly men slip daily. To these convictions, he is able to add immense theatrical gifts. He knows how to make a point simple and obvious, how to give it bite in the illustration and how to make language ring out from the stage. He has not only the professional crusader's zeal for humanity, but the imaginative writer's feel for it.

"Mood plays" dismay Miller. "The pretense," he says, "is that nobody wrote them—they were just there." And he has no patience with what he sees as the present schism between philosophy and politics; his ultimate purpose is to weld them together as the Greeks and Elizabethans did. He has pointed out that Shakespeare and Sophocles had one thing in common: they both tried ". . . to draw a whole world into one man, to bring a national experience to bear on an individual subject."

Miller's plea is that we re-examine the premises by which we live. Each new work is meant to hasten the day when the present equation, man versus society, will give place to the ideal equation, man equals society. He sees the theater as a place where people must be made to think, as well as to be entertained. Though Miller's deep involvement with social issues is evident throughout his work, he is still basically a playwright and as such finds his greatest satisfaction. He has called his work, ". . . the only normal trade for a sensible man." A friend once observed that "For Arthur, an ivory tower is an uninhabitable slum." And, by Miller's own admission, he is driven to write by a sleepless social conscience.

Introduction to *The Crucible*

A "crucible" is a severe test, or a trial. It is also a container that can withstand great heat. As it passes through a furnace, the metals and ores within it are transformed in some way. For the characters in *The Crucible*, the Salem witch hunt is the trial from which they emerge utterly changed. As each character passes through the furnace of lies, vengeance, greed and torture, he is either purified or corrupted. For John Proctor, the heat is especially intense, and the struggle toward goodness is laden with many traps and obstacles.

All the characters in *The Crucible* are based on real persons who lived in Salem in 1692. For dramatic purposes, several characters have sometimes been fused into one and small details have been changed. In general, however, the actions of the characters are closely matched to the actions of their historical counterparts. Miller researched the period exhaustively and wanted his play to be as true to the historical records as possible. See Appendix I for some of these records.

Although *The Crucible* offers many parallels with our own time, it also makes use of many ideas and attitudes that were unique to Salem, Massachusetts, in 1692. Some knowledge of life in Salem is needed to fully understand the play. The following material, therefore, explains basic Puritan customs and beliefs, and offers a summary of the actual Salem witch hunt. In addition, this introduction looks at Miller's use of the witch hunt to comment on the McCarthy hearings of the 1950s.

The Puritans

In 1620, the Puritans landed at Plymouth Rock in Massachusetts and founded the first permanent settlement in New England. They had left England to escape religious persecution and to establish a New Jerusalem in the New World. This Promised Land, however, contained many new dangers. In the face of a harsh climate, fierce animals, hostile Indians and a vast, godless wilderness, the Puritans drew together in a tightly unified group with extremely strict rules and an autocratic leadership. Through a combination of bitterly hard work, rigid discipline and harsh justice, the Puritans succeeded in taming the land that no one before them could conquer.

The Puritan government was a theocracy; that is, it was

completely controlled by the Puritan church. The ministers of the church were also the town officers and administrators. Because the Puritans believed that they were the new Chosen People, they did not permit members of any other religion to corrupt their pure society. Those who did not belong to the church could not hold property or vote. In addition, those who did not attend church regularly or follow the church regulations could be excommunicated, thereby losing all their property and rights.

In *The Crucible*, Deputy Governor Danforth is the perfect example of a theocratic ruler. Because he believes that he speaks for God, he cannot accept the possibility that he has been wrong. In his ruthless judgments, he holds to the strict letter of the law, for "While I speak God's law, I will not crack its voice with whimpering."

"God's law" for the Puritans was certainly strict. Anything that distracted them from hard work was part of the Devil's plan to destroy them. There were no celebrations or holidays, no theaters or novels and no children's games or entertainments. Dancing was considered a serious sin. It was natural, then, that Abigail and the other girls felt a need to dance in the woods. Their youthful high spirits had no other outlet. It was also natural that they should lie to cover up their "sin." If they had been found out, they would probably have been whipped.

In addition to viewing pleasure as sinful, the Puritans saw sex as a necessary evil, to be practised joylessly only between a man and his wife. As John Proctor knew only too well, adultery was considered a hideous crime and could easily result in excommunication and the loss of one's property. Some historical analysts believe that this sexual repression was directly responsible for the mass hysteria that produced the witch hunt. In *The Crucible*, Abigail's dislike for the people of Salem is largely based on her contempt for this repression.

The Puritans believed that everything stated in the Bible was literally true. The Devil was very real to them, always trying to tempt them away from their work and God's laws. Moreover, the Devil was a cunning and extremely powerful opponent. Once he set out to destroy a soul, there was almost nothing the person could do to prevent it. As Abigail angrily tells Deputy Governor Danforth: "Think you to be so mighty that the power of Hell may not turn *your* wits? Beware of it!"

This grim sense of man's powerlessness was also found in other aspects of Puritan life. The Puritans believed in the doctrine of the elect. According to this fatalistic belief, only a few people would be chosen by God to be saved from Hell. There was nothing a person could do to earn a place among the elect. No amount of good works or righteous living could help. All a person could do was live an upright life in the blind hope that he might be one of the few who were chosen.

A major reason why salvation was so difficult to attain is found in the Puritans' adaptation of the doctrine of original sin. According to the Puritans, each person at birth is already evil and on the verge of eternal damnation. As Jonathan Edwards, a famed Puritan minister, once preached, "The God that holds you over the pit of Hell, much as one holds a spider, or some loathsome insect, over the fire, abhors you, and is dreadfully provoked; his wrath towards you burns like fire; he looks upon you as worthy of nothing else, but to be cast into the fire . . . ." In *The Crucible*, Parris also preached "hellfire and bloody damnation" in his sermons, much to Proctor's disgust.

Not only was man born an evil sinner, but his sins could not be washed away. Therefore, every person concealed guilt in his heart from which he could never be free. In *The Crucible*, John Proctor is deeply troubled with guilt as a result of his adulterous affair with Abigail. He tries to bury this guilt by pretending it doesn't exist. Nonetheless, as Elizabeth tells him, "The magistrate sits in your heart that judges you."

Although their guilt could never be entirely removed, it was sometimes possible for Puritans who sinned to regain the path of righteousness. First, however, they had to publicly confess their sins and perform some act of penance. This policy of open confession was carried to absurd lengths during the witch hunt. Those accused of witchcraft could either confess to lies or hang. Not surprisingly, most chose to confess.

Because the Puritans' legal system was used to uphold religious laws, many such absurdities were possible. Over the centuries, Western society has developed "due process of law" so that the truth can be uncovered. This due process uses witnesses and other hard evidence to prove whether a person is innocent or guilty. The accused is also granted certain rights so that he can defend himself. The Puritans, however, could not rely on due process to get at the truth. Because religious crimes involved magic and invisibility, there could be no witnesses or hard evidence.

In *The Crucible*, Deputy Governor Danforth sums up the absurdity of the Puritan court when he explains that witchcraft is an invisible crime. Only the witch and her victim can possibly witness this crime, and the witch would never accuse herself. Therefore, the victim's testimony must always be accurate. As a result of this absurd reasoning, the Puritans had no way of objectively finding out the truth. When the lack of due process was combined with the false confessions, the door was opened to a reign of terror in which rumors, lies and superstitions ruled the courts.

In summary, then, virtually every aspect of a Puritan's life fell under the strict control of the church. Rigid discipline was enforced, and pleasures were forbidden. Personal rights were few and could be suspended at any time. Personal freedoms were virtually non-existent. Life for the early Puritans was a constant battle against the harsh climate, the vast wilderness and the temptations of Satan. Even for those who won that battle, divine salvation was by no means guaranteed.

By 1692, however, the land had been partly tamed and the surrounding wilderness was no longer so terrifying. The need for rigid discipline, hard work and tight unity was no longer as great as it had been. To the great concern of the church, many Puritans began to feel the need for more personal rights and freedoms. Ultimately, the church's struggle to maintain its authority against ever-increasing opposition erupted into the full-blown hysteria of the Salem witch hunt.

Witchcraft Among the Puritans

The persecution of witches was by no means limited to the Puritans in New England. During the 17th and early 18th centuries, tens of thousands of people were executed as witches throughout Europe and the Americas. The Roman Catholic Inquisition was especially bloodthirsty in its relentless pursuit of those who practised the black arts.

It is not surprising that the fear of witchcraft took so deep a hold among the New England Puritans. As fundamentalists, they believed every word that was written in the Bible. Moses' statement, "Thou shalt not suffer a witch to live," was well known by almost every member of the colony. In *The Crucible*, when Elizabeth Proctor suggests that witches do not exist, Reverend Hale scolds her, "You surely do not fly against the Gospel, the Gospel —."

The Puritans deeply believed in evil as a tangible force in the world. The Devil was a real being, the lord of the angels cast out of heaven for betraying God. Since his fall, the Devil had worked constantly to destroy God's kingdom on earth by tempting God's subjects away from Him.

Because the Puritans believed that their colony was the center of God's earthly kingdom, they believed that the Devil was focusing all his attention on their destruction. The vast wilderness around them provided the Devil with many hiding places, as well as many heathen savages who willingly did his work. According to Puritan belief, once the colony was perfected the Devil would be banished forever. Because he knew this, he was attacking them now with all his power and might.

The Puritans, then, considered themselves soldiers in the midst of a great war against evil. The enemy was powerful, and capable of infinite deception. As Reverend Hale claims, "Until an hour before the Devil fell, God thought him beautiful in Heaven." Human beings, on the other hand, were weak, born in sin and likely destined for damnation. To make matters even worse, the Devil had recruited many helpers among the Puritans themselves. These helpers were known as witches.

The belief in witchcraft is very ancient and can be found in almost all cultures. In general, a witch is a person who is believed to have supernatural powers. In many cultures, witches have been revered as wisewomen or healers. In others, they have been persecuted and killed.

As modern feminists point out, almost all of those who have been killed as witches have been women. Often these women directly challenged male authority. Many had become influential in their villages through the practice of midwifery or herbal medicine. Witchcraft has always been associated with the dark, irrational side of human nature, a side traditionally seen as female. In addition, many of the rituals associated with witchcraft are highly sexual in nature. Feminists argue that female sexuality is considered most threatening by male-dominated, sexually-repressed societies. Certainly, no more sexually-repressed a society has ever existed than that of the Puritans.

The Puritans were never really clear on exactly how witches helped the Devil in his battle for human souls. Apparently, a person became a witch by making an agreement with the Devil. The witch then "sent out" her invisible spirit to harm innocent people. Sometimes a witch entered an innocent person's body and controlled his thoughts. A witch could also assume the shape of an innocent person while tormenting others, thereby framing the innocent person for crimes he didn't commit.

Needless to say, all this resulted in a fair amount of legal confusion when charges against witches were laid. As Danforth pointed out, witchcraft was impossible to prove even with witnesses or hard evidence. In general, the word of the victim was taken, even though it was recognized that the Devil's trickery may have caused an innocent person to be accused.

The absurdities do not end there. Any witch could end her contract with Satan simply by confessing to witchcraft. Since hanging was generally the alternative, many witches did indeed confess. Yet, presumably, a real witch would have no qualms about lying while pretending to confess. Meanwhile, a truly devout Puritan, such as Rebecca Nurse, would be unable to make a dishonest confession, and would therefore hang. In other words, the laws on witchcraft were such that the least devout Puritans lived while the most devout, who refused to lie, were hung.

In 1692, the Puritans believed that they had found the Devil's center of attack in Salem, Massachusetts. As a result of the legal absurdities outlined above, the courts were turned over to hysteria, private vengeance and land greed. In what was to become known as "the delusion," hundreds were arrested for witchcraft, and 20 innocent people lost their lives.

The Salem Witch Hunt

Salem does not seem to have ever been a very peaceful village. Long before the witch hunt, the people in the town had split into opposing factions as a result of land feuds and political disagreement. Because boundaries were somewhat unsettled, different claims were often made to the same tract of land.

In particular, a longstanding quarrel had developed between the Nurses and the Putnams, two of the largest and wealthiest families in the district. Various wills and deeds were contested in court through a long series of lawsuits. Over time, the quarrel grew as friends and distant relatives of both families took sides against one another.

This conflict was made more intense when Reverend Parris defeated the Putnams' candidate to be elected as minister of Salem. Because Parris did not have a clear majority, his election was contested. Parris also angered many members of his congregation with his requests for free firewood, expensive church additions and the deed to the minister's home.

Reverend Parris had a black servant, named Tituba, whom he had found in Barbados. Tituba's customs were considered strange and dangerous by the solemn Puritan townspeople. Eventually, she was caught teaching Parris' daughter, Betty, and niece, Abigail Williams, how to tell the future by reading palms. Tituba was punished, but the suspicion of witchcraft was firmly planted in the minds of the Salemites.

In February, 1692, Betty Parris began to suffer from some sort of fit. The doctors were baffled by her illness and suggested that it had a supernatural cause. Reverend Parris sent for the help of other ministers, and he tried to keep his daughter's illness hidden from the town. Word spread, however, and before long rumors of witchcraft were flying through Salem.

No one knows precisely what happened next. However, on February 29, 1692, the first three arrests for witchcraft were made. At this stage, the accused were all social outcasts. Tituba was a black servant from another country. Sarah Good was an old beggarwoman. And Sarah Osborne seldom attended church and was considered immoral.

These three women were ordered to either confess to witchcraft or hang. Not surprisingly, they confessed. In their confessions, they were forced to accuse other Salemites of doing Satan's work. Before long, the jails were full of prisoners accused of witchcraft.

The role of Abigail Williams, Betty Parris, Mary Warren and others in these events is not quite clear. Quite possibly, Abigail and Betty made the first accusations against Tituba, Sarah Good and Sarah Osborne. Certainly, they made a number of later accusations, and many innocent people were found guilty as a result of the girls' testimony.

The witchcraft trials took place in Salem while the governor of Massachusetts was absent on a campaign against the Indians.

In his place, Lieutenant Governor William Stroughton acted as chief justice. Stroughton was a strict Puritan who followed the law to the letter, and he totally believed in the existence of witchcraft. Like Danforth in *The Crucible*, he could not bear to have his authority questioned. Stroughton issued the first death warrant in Salem and personally witnessed the hanging that resulted.

The Salem trials began in March, 1692. For evidence, the court relied on the testimony of the young girls and on the confessions of those who were threatened with hanging. During the trials, 55 people confessed to being witches. The first hanging took place in June. Five others were hung on July 19, five on August 19, and eight on September 22. During this time, Giles Corey was pressed to death for refusing to plead guilty or not guilty. In addition, two dogs were hung as witches.

By October, 150 prisoners were still awaiting trial, and others had already been condemned to die. Many of these prisoners were highly respectable men and women whose arrests had raised a public outcry. The public had also been enraged by rumors that some important men had used their influence to prevent their wives' arrests, while others had bribed the court to find their wives innocent. Salemites began to doubt the testimony of the young girls and question the false confessions.

Governor Phips ordered the court to find a more trustworthy method of testing for witchcraft than the testimony of the girls. A series of meetings resulted with some ministers protesting the lack of hard evidence and rejecting the use of the forced confessions. Finally, on October 29, 1692, Governor Phips yielded to public pressure and put an end to the trials and executions.

The witch hunt continued to affect the lives of the people of Salem long after the last trial was over. Twenty Salemites were dead and their property confiscated. Many others had been excommunicated, and had lost their property and rights as a result.

Not until 1709, 17 years after the trials, did the survivors and the heirs of the victims feel free to ask the government for restitution. In 1711, some money was awarded as compensation. However, much of this money was given to informers rather than to victims or their heirs. The reputations of the accused were reinstated and, in 1712, the excommunications were reversed by government order.

As Miller notes at the end of *The Crucible*, some of the farms that had belonged to the accused witches were left to ruin for more than a century before anyone would dare to live in them again.

McCarthyism and *The Crucible*

After World War II, America and Russia began to view one another uneasily. The two countries were based on opposing ideologies, namely capitalism and communism. In addition, each country was rapidly expanding its political influence throughout Europe and the Third World. In 1947, the Cold War began, and the two powers began to treat one another as deadly enemies. In America, anyone who had ever flirted with socialist or communist beliefs was suddenly seen as a traitor to the American way of life.

Although the persecution of leftists took its name from the McCarthy hearings of the early 1950s, it actually began with the publication of the Attorney-General's List in 1947 by the House Committee of Un-American Activities (HUAC). This list contained names of people with ties to subversive or communist organizations. Later, this list expanded to become the notorious Black List, by which thousands of people were forbidden to work in their professions. In addition, HUAC held hearings to investigate charges of "Un-Americanism." These hearings continued through the McCarthy era and were often more damaging than the McCarthy hearings themselves.

In 1950, the Chinese Revolution had just been won, the Russians had exploded their first atomic bomb and the Korean War had just begun. The time was ripe for an explosion of anti-communist feeling. Overnight, Senator Joseph McCarthy became famous with his accusation that, for 20 years, the Democratic government had been nurturing the growth of communism in America. Under McCarthy, Senate hearings were set up and the wholesale persecution of leftists began.

It should be remembered that during the Spanish Civil War and World War II, many people had worked with socialists and leftists to fight fascism. Indeed, only a few years before, America and Russia had been allies. Under McCarthyism, however, anti-communist hysteria became so intense and so irrational that even moderate liberals referred to it as a witch hunt. As Miller states in his notes to *The Crucible*, "in America any man who is not reactionary in his views is open to the charge of alliance with the Red hell . . . a political policy is equated with moral right, and opposition to it with diabolical malevolence."

The McCarthy and HUAC hearings followed a similar pattern. As each "witness" took the stand, he would be asked whether he had ever had any dealings with communists. If he refused to answer, he could be arrested. If he denied the charge, he would be asked to prove his innocence by giving the names of those who did have communist connections. If he confessed to having once attended a leftist meeting or contributed to a leftist cause, then he was asked to show that he had reformed by naming others who had attended that meeting or worked for that cause. Those who were named were then called to the hearings as new witnesses.

Unfortunately, few witnesses had the courage to stand up to the McCarthy and HUAC committees. Most willingly gave the names of friends and colleagues who had at some time been associated with leftist causes. If they didn't know any names, they often repeated rumors or simply lied. And, as one critic commented in disgust, "they lied, not to save their lives, but to save their swimming pools."

The McCarthy hearings particularly focused on the arts in America. Between 1950 and 1954, several artists and intellectuals were imprisoned for refusing to testify, including Dashiell Hammett and the famous "Hollywood Ten." In addition, thousands of writers, musicians, actors and directors were "blacklisted" and forbidden to work. Some left the country, others changed professions, and still others changed their names. Some resumed their careers when the blacklist was lifted in the 1960s, but for most the damage was permanent.

Eventually, McCarthy's power collapsed under its own weight. As the government and the arts were purged over and over, the old lists became tired and worn. McCarthy became wilder and wilder in his accusations, claiming that the American army had become disloyal and that powerful generals were traitors. The public became increasingly skeptical of McCarthy's charges and began to press for the truth. Public opposition increased as a number of well-known witnesses, including Arthur Miller, challenged the authority of the HUAC and McCarthy hearings.

The Crucible was first performed in January of 1953. It

must have seemed like a slap in the face to McCarthy by a leading American playwright. McCarthyism had been called a witch hunt, and here was a play about the real witch hunt. Parallels between the Salem court and the McCarthy and HUAC hearings were clearly drawn.

During the hearings, as in Salem, due process of law was abandoned and hysteria was spread through lies and rumors. Witnesses were trapped into dishonest confessions and forced to falsely accuse their friends and neighbors. Those who opposed the hearings were accused of working for the Red devil, rather than simply the Devil, as in Salem. In Washington, as in Salem, many innocent people suffered. As Miller says of the victims of the witch hunt, "one can only pity them all, just as we will be pitied someday."

Today, the Salem witch hunt is far behind us and the McCarthy era too is history. Nonetheless, *The Crucible* still has political meaning for our time. In his notes to *The Crucible*, Miller points out that "the balance has yet to be struck between order and freedom." Every age and every society has its repressions. In the past few years, members of the "Moral Majority" have increasingly tried to limit various freedoms in the United States. Quite possibly, Americans will soon have to choose once more between authority of the state and freedom of the individual.

The Crucible's themes, then, are timeless. As long as governments continue to distort the truth, individuals with courage and integrity will continue to challenge them. The choice between freedom and repression is always with us.

Plot Summary

The first act of *The Crucible*, subtitled "An Overture," is set in a small, austerely furnished bedroom at Reverend Samuel Parris' house in Salem, Massachusetts. The year is 1692. The Reverend is on his knees, praying at the foot of his 10-year-old daughter's bed, while the girl, Betty, lies inert. Although his prayers alternate with weeping and mumbling, she does not stir. Presently, Tituba, the Negro slave Parris had brought back from Barbados, enters. She is devoted to Betty. Parris orders her out of the room despite her concern for his daughter. It is evident that he is overcome by fear at the child's strange malady. He is trying to waken her when his niece, 17-year-old Abigail Williams, enters to tell him that Susanna Walcott, a village girl, has arrived with word from Dr. Griggs. Susanna tells Parris that the doctor has been unable to find any clue in his books as to Betty's ailment, and has therefore suggested that the Reverend look to "unnatural things."

Before Susanna leaves, Abigail cautions her to say nothing about this to any of the villagers. Abigail then tells her uncle that the rumor of witchcraft is sweeping Salem, and that his house is packed with people who are waiting downstairs for his denial that his daughter is, in fact, bewitched. At this, Parris grows more frightened, and tells his niece that he had seen her and Betty dancing in the moonlight "like heathen in the forest" while Tituba watched. He presses her to admit that they were trafficking with spirits. And, he adds that he must know why she was discharged from service at the Proctor home. It has been said that Elizabeth Proctor attends church so infrequently because she refuses to sit next to "something soiled."

Abigail is quick to retort that Goody Proctor is a bitter, lying woman who hates her only because she would not slave for her. When Parris asks why no one else has called for Abigail's service in the seven months since she left the Proctors', she haughtily tells him that she will slave for no one, and calls Elizabeth a gossiping liar who has sullied her name.

They are interrupted by the arrival of Mrs. Ann Putnam, a superstitious gossip, who immediately tells Parris that a "stroke of hell" is upon his house, and demands to know how high Betty has flown. She has already decided that Betty is, in fact, a witch, and claims that Betty has been seen flying around the town. When Thomas, her husband, arrives and confirms this, Parris' fears reach their peak. He is struck dumb that the Putnams' daughter, Ruth, is also strangely ill.

At this point, Abigail turns to Parris and whispers that not she, but Ruth and Tituba had conjured spirits. "I am undone!" he cries, but Thomas Putnam reminds him that an admission of having discovered witchcraft in his house will clear him.

They are joined by Mercy Lewis, the Putnams' 18-year-old servant, who is left alone with Abigail and Betty after the Putnams leave and the Reverend goes downstairs to lead the towns-people in a psalm while they await Reverend Hale. Abigail takes charge immediately and gives orders to Mercy: she is to admit only that they danced, as Abigail had already confessed to that sin. Parris had seen Mercy naked, and knew that Tituba had conjured Ruth's sisters out of their graves.

Mary Warren, the Proctors' 17-year-old servant, enters and turns to Abigail for advice. She is in a state of panic, and begs Abigail to tell the truth: they had only been dancing, a sin punishable by whipping, whereas witchery is a "hangin' error." Abigail shakes Betty until she sits up, and then comments sarcastically upon her improvement. She says that she has told Parris everything. At this, Betty leaps out of bed and flattens herself against the wall. She cries that she saw Abigail drink blood as a charm to kill John Proctor's wife. Abigail slaps Betty's face and warns her never to mention this again.

Abigail, who is clearly the leader, warns them that her power of revenge will fall upon them if they breathe a word of anything but the dancing and the conjurings of Tituba. Then, John Proctor arrives, looking for Mary, who he has forbidden to leave his house. His presence alters the mood in the room. Mercy sidles out after Mary, leaving Proctor alone with Abigail, and Betty once more prone on her bed. He tells Abigail of the town's mumblings about witchcraft, and she replies that they were merely dancing in the woods.

The sound of a psalm is heard from downstairs, and Betty suddenly claps her hands to her ears and begins to scream. Proctor is unnerved, and Parris, the Putnams and Mercy return to the room. As they try to quiet Betty, Mrs. Putnam exclaims that all this is a mark of witchcraft.

Parris fights with Corey and Proctor over his firewood allotment. Putnam in turn provokes an argument with Proctor over a long-standing grudge about some of Proctor's land that Putnam considers rightfully his. Rebecca remains mild and conciliatory. At the height of this bickering, Reverend John Hale arrives.

Hale is a serious man of 40, who looks upon his errand with pride, for at last he is considered authority enough on witchcraft to be called for consultation on the subject to which he has devoted most of his life.

When Hale turns his attention to Abigail, she quickly grasps her opportunity, and accuses Tituba of forcing her and Betty to deal with the Devil and of sending her spirit out to them. The terrified slave is brought in, hysterically denying the accusation, but it is useless. In a frenzy of fear, she finally admits that she did indeed talk to the Devil, and that he in turn had told her the names of *white* people with whom he worked. Betty joins her in hysterical relief and the two girls call out names faster and faster. Hale sends Putnam for the marshal.

Act II begins eight days later, in the home of John and Elizabeth Proctor. The mood here is in sharp contrast to that of the previous act. The Proctors are gentle and polite to each other, but there seems to be a strain between them. Elizabeth tells her husband that Mary Warren has gone into Salem as an "official of the court." Proctor is astonished to learn that not only has a court been set up, but that 14 women have been jailed as witches. Moreover, Deputy Governor Danforth has sworn to hang them if they do not confess. The town has gone wild and, as Abigail has now established herself as the girls' leader, she is treated with great deference. The Proctors agree that it is John's duty to go to the court and tell them that, by Abigail's own admission to him, the accusations are fraudulent. The cause of the gulf between the Proctors becomes clear when John tells his wife that he had been alone with the girl when she admitted the lies. Proctor had told Elizabeth of his past affair with Abigail, but has been uneasy with her ever since.

The Proctors become more and more horrified as they hear how the words of honest women were turned against them. They also learn that pregnant women are safe until the birth of the child. Finally, Proctor can stand no more and, as Mary brags about her new status as an official, he threatens to whip her. At this, Mary, drunk with power, points to his wife and says that she, too, had been accused, but that Mary had saved

17

her life. The identity of her accuser is secret, but the Proctors realize that it is Abigail, who hopes to have Elizabeth hanged in order to take her place as John's wife.

Suddenly, Reverend Hale appears. His manner has changed from one of assurance to one of deference, almost guilt. He has come to tell Elizabeth that she has been accused and is about to be taken to jail. He questions the Proctors about their slackened church attendance. Proctor explains that he considers Reverend Parris a self-advancing hypocrite rather than a true man of God. Hale asks Proctor to recite the commandments, but he falters over "Thou shalt not commit adultery." Finally, Proctor tells Hale of Abigail's admission to him that there was no witchcraft, just dancing in the woods. Reverend Hale's doubts grow and, when Giles Corey and Francis Nurse rush in to say that their wives have been taken to jail, his doubts become convictions.

Marshal Herrick and a neighbor, Ezekiel Cheever, arrive. The latter, a tailor, has been made a court clerk and has a warrant for the arrest of Elizabeth Proctor and 15 others. Abigail had indeed accused her, claiming that Elizabeth had bewitched the poppet given to her by Mary Warren. It had caused Abigail to fall down screaming from a needle sticking into her belly. The doll is examined, and is found to have a needle stuck into it. When Mary is called, she remembers that Abigail sat next to her when she was making the doll. In a rage, Proctor accuses Abigail of deliberately sticking herself, tears the warrant up, and tries to throw Herrick and Cheever out. He turns upon Hale and asks if he will allow Elizabeth to be taken. Hale falteringly replies that the court is just.

The Salem meeting house, now converted into a court, is the scene of the third act. An inquisition of the women by Judge Hathorne and Deputy Governor Danforth has been taking place. Giles Corey, frantic with concern for his wife, is overridden by Hathorne's implacable belief in the signs of her guilt and Danforth's zeal for justice. Corey attempts to show that Putnam is accusing people so that he may get their land. He is told to name the man who had told him this, but he refuses in order to keep the man out of jail.

When John Proctor enters with Mary Warren, Danforth tells him that his wife is pregnant, and therefore safe for a year. Although Elizabeth has been saved, Proctor insists, in the name of justice, that Mary speak her piece. She tells Danforth, tearfully, that she lied, that Abigail was responsible for the needle in the poppet. Then, Susanna, Mercy, Betty and Abigail are brought in to confront her. Abigail says she is lying, and Mary begins to weaken. Still, she admits to having seen no spirits and to having pretended when she testified.

Abigail, trapped, gathers all her resources and suddenly turns on Mary. She begins to shiver, saying that she is being bewitched by Mary, and then falls to the ground. Proctor leaps at her and pulls her up, but is restrained by Parris and Hathorne. Maddened with rage, he calls her a whore, and confesses to having slept with her eight months before, and to having lusted for her since then.

As Elizabeth is led into the room, the others are told to turn their backs. When Elizabeth is asked why she dismissed Abigail, she answers that she was jealous of her. Did John Proctor ever commit the crime of lechery to her knowledge? No, she replies. Proctor cries out to her to tell the truth, but she is removed from the room immediately.

Abigail now falls down again, screaming that a bird is on the ceiling, which is Mary's spirit threatening to attack her. The other girls fall into this easily enough, and the terrified Mary turns on Proctor, recanting once more by saying that he had threatened to murder her if she did not testify as he wished. Hale now fully perceives the horror of what has been happening and, as both John Proctor and Giles Corey are being taken off to jail, he denounces the proceedings to Danforth and shouts that he is finished with the court. The door slams behind him.

The final act takes place in the Salem jail. It appears that Hale, in an agony of remorse, has been going among the condemned women and praying with them. Meanwhile, Reverend Parris has discovered that Mercy Lewis and Abigail have robbed his strongbox and fled. He, too, is beginning to have doubts. Rebecca Nurse and John Proctor, two of the most respected townspeople, are condemned to hang, which makes him uneasy. He proposes to the deputy governor that the executions be postponed, but Danforth is adamant. Hale enters to tell them that Rebecca has refused to confess, but that he has not spoken to John Proctor. Parris suggests that they arrange for the Proctors to meet; perhaps the sight of his pregnant wife will cause him to confess and go free. Elizabeth is brought in with her wrists chained, and Hale tells her that unless John confesses, he will die at sunrise. He implores her to beg her husband to recant, but she remains silent. At last, she asks to speak to John and he is ushered in, in chains. They are left alone, facing each other.

Hathorne returns and Proctor tells him that he wants to live and will confess. Danforth, Cheever, Parris and Hale rush in at this news, and pen and paper are brought quickly. As Proctor begins his confession, Rebecca Nurse, supported by Herrick, is led in because Danforth wishes her to witness the example set by Proctor. But she refuses to damn herself by lying. And, when Proctor is asked to name the people that he saw with the Devil, he refuses. Hale, anxious to get it over with, asks that Danforth sign the paper on the basis of the confession alone, but Proctor's signature is needed first. Protesting that their witness to his testimony should be sufficient, Proctor refuses at first to sign, and Danforth refuses to certify an unsigned confession. Proctor then signs it, but snatches the paper away the moment that he has done so. He will not have this paper nailed to the church door on the day that good people are being hanged for their silence. "You will hang!" they cry, and Proctor's eyes fill with tears as Elizabeth rushes to him. He shouts, as he holds her, that he sees some shreds of goodness in himself yet. As he and Rebecca are taken out to be hanged, Parris and Hale continue to plead with Elizabeth to stop him. "He has his goodness now. God forbid I take it from him!" she cries, as the final drumroll crashes, and the play ends.

Characters in the Play

Ezekiel Cheever: A tailor. He is made court clerk during the trials, and becomes inflated with his own importance.

Giles Corey: A bent but still powerful man of 83, he is canny, inquisitive and not easily led.

Deputy Governor Danforth: A grave, stern man in his sixties, who is devoted to his cause. He will let nothing interfere with the performance of his duties. He is, nevertheless, a sophisticated man with a strain of humor.

Sarah Good: An old beggarwoman, who is thrown into jail before she knows what has happened to her.

Reverend John Hale: An intellectual, self-searching man of 40. He is concerned with the power of the Devil, and has done much reading on the subject. He is thin and tight-skinned, with eager eyes.

Judge Hathorne: He is a typical Salem judge, bitter and remorseless.

Marshal Herrick: He is in charge of arresting all of the accused witches.

Hopkins: A jail guard.

Mercy Lewis: The Putnams' servant, a fat, sly girl of 18.

Francis Nurse: He commands respect as a fair arbiter of disputes. He is a good man, in his seventies, and a successful farmer.

Rebecca Nurse: The kindly and wise wife of Francis Nurse, who is later accused of being a witch.

Betty Parris: The ten-year-old daughter of Reverend Parris. She is impressionable, and has never had much attention paid to her.

Reverend Samuel Parris: A harsh, stern man in his mid-forties. He has a persecution complex, and is both disliked and feared.

Elizabeth Proctor: John Proctor's wife, a good woman, straightforward and honest.

John Proctor: A farmer in his middle thirties. He has little patience with fools or hypocrites. He is intelligent, deliberate and manly.

Mrs. Ann Putnam: A 45-year-old woman; a vicious gossip, who is easy prey to suggestion and superstition. She is obsessed with dreams and visions of devils and witches.

Thomas Putnam: Ann's husband, a prosperous landowner of almost 50. He is embroiled in disputes over land that does not belong to him, but which he is greedy to obtain.

Tituba: The Negro slave of the Reverend Parris. She is a native of Barbados, and finds the strange, repressed ways of the Puritans incomprehensible.

Susanna Walcott: A nervous and harried girl of about 16.

Mary Warren: A not-too-bright girl of 17; servant of the Proctors. She is friendless and naive.

Abigail Williams: A beautiful girl of 17, orphaned, and a niece of Parris. She is calculating, vicious and dissatisfied with life. She is obsessed with desire for John Proctor.

Summaries and Commentaries by Act and Scene

Note: The acts in *The Crucible* are not divided into scenes, because the events take place at only one time and location in each act. However, for the sake of clarity each act has been divided into what Arthur Miller has called its "indivisible dramatic units." These "scenes" generally begin and end with the entrance or exit of major characters.

ACT I • SCENE 1

Summary

Act I takes place in the sparsely furnished bedroom of Betty Parris, the ten-year-old daughter of Reverend Samuel Parris. The year is 1692, and the town is Salem, Massachusetts. Betty is lying still on her bed while her father prays desperately for her to get well. Parris' servant from Barbados, Tituba, enters fearfully and is ordered away from the bedside. Parris' niece and ward, Abigail Williams, also enters, along with Susanna, who delivers a message from the doctor that Betty's illness probably results from unnatural causes. Susanna then leaves.

Parris is very worried. The night before, he had discovered Betty, Abigail, Tituba and other girls dancing naked in the woods. Abigail denies that witchcraft was involved or that the girls took off their clothes. She also tells Parris that she had been fired some months earlier from her position as servant by Elizabeth Proctor through no fault of her own. Parris continues to worry, as much for his reputation as minister as for his daughter's health.

The Putnams arrive, and quickly show themselves to be superstitious, self-righteous and malicious. The Putnams had lost seven babies which they believed had been murdered by witchcraft. In the woods the night before, their daughter, Ruth Putnam, had been casting spells with Tituba and the other girls to find out the murderer's name. Since then, Ruth, like Betty, had been seized with an unnatural illness. Mrs. Putnam also claims that Betty has been seen flying on a broom.

Abigail admits that Ruth and Tituba had been "conjuring spirits." Putnam urges Parris to go downstairs and confess to the growing crowd that he had discovered witchcraft in his house. Parris refuses, but agrees to lead the crowd in a psalm.

The scene ends as Parris and the Putnams exit.

Commentary

While setting the stage for the first scene, Arthur Miller takes the chance to discuss the nature of Puritan society. To help them survive against the hostile wilderness that surrounded them, the Puritans had formed a closely knit, highly unified society with a theocratic government that blended state and religious power. Religious laws and state laws were the same, and both were strictly enforced. This close unity did indeed help the Puritans to survive and prosper, though it suppressed individual freedoms. By the time of the Salem witch hunts in 1692, however, the wilderness had largely been tamed, and more and more Puritans had begun to demand greater personal liberty. According to Miller, the witch hunt resulted from the panic that set in as the old theocratic structure became seriously challenged by a demand for new freedoms.

The witch hunt allowed long-repressed sexual desires to come to the surface in hysterical stories of rape by spirits. The witch hunt also allowed people like the Putnams, who were involved in long-standing feuds over property, to take their revenge. Old hatreds could now be settled once and for all.

As Miller points out, "it is still impossible for man to organize his social life without repressions." The old conflict between individual freedom and state-ruled conformity is still with us. In America, that conflict reached its peak in the McCarthy era of the late 1940s and early 1950s. During that period, many Americans, including Miller, were accused of being communists and were forced to either accuse others or abandon their careers. Many Americans were imprisoned on little or no evidence.

Miller uses Scene 1 to set the stage for the entire play, and to introduce many of his themes. We quickly learn that this is a society in which power and morality have become repressive and confused. The minister, the town's center of Christian authority, is more concerned for his reputation than for his seriously ill daughter. That reputation is largely at the mercy of powerful landowners like the Putnams, whose view of the world is tainted with malice, suspicion and superstition.

24

In Salem, the individual freedoms that other societies take for granted do not exist. There is little privacy: everyone minds everyone else's business, no one knocks on doors, and rumors spread like wildfire. Harmless pleasures are seen as dark and sinful. Young girls must sneak off into the woods to dance, and they must later tell crazy lies to cover up their activities.

As Parris leaves his daughter's room, he turns to Putnam and says of Betty, "There is a terrible power in her arms today." He means physical power. In her hysteria, Betty has already tried to jump from the window. But Betty also holds other kinds of power in her arms. The Putnams claim that she is infected with the Devil's power, the power of witchcraft. Certainly, at this point, Betty holds the power of life and death over the many who will be tried as witches as a result of the lies she is about to tell. This play on the word "power" illustrates a central theme of the play: when political power is based on superstition and hysteria, society becomes corrupt.

ACT I • SCENE 2

Summary
Abigail and Betty are left alone with Mercy, the Putnams' maid. The two girls are frightened because all Salem has been talking of witchcraft. Mary Warren, the Proctors' maid, enters, also frightened. Abigail orders the other girls to confess to nothing more than dancing. Betty awakes and hysterically runs for the window. She accuses Abigail of drinking blood to cast a spell and kill Elizabeth Proctor. Abigail slaps her, and threatens her and the others with a horrible revenge if they do not keep silent.

Abigail stops speaking as John Proctor enters.

Commentary
The Puritan ethic involved strict sexual repression. In this scene, the girls reveal that they have been acting out their sexual frustrations by dancing naked in the woods and taking part in Tituba's voodoo rituals. Now they are terrified. Their behavior has violated several Puritan taboos. For just dancing, the girls will be whipped and their reputations will be tarnished. If their nakedness is discovered, they will be seriously punished and branded as harlots for the rest of their lives. And for witchcraft, they will hang.

This scene tells us a great deal about Abigail. She is a natural leader: she decides the group's strategies and easily bullies Betty and Mary. She is ruthless: she saw her parents die violently, and her threats ring true. She is self-serving: she decides to accuse the absent Ruth and Tituba of witchcraft to save herself. She is dishonest: she has lied to her uncle about her actions in the woods and pretended a concern for Betty that clearly she doesn't feel. And she is vengeful: she has cast a spell against the same Elizabeth Proctor who fired her as a maid. As the play unfolds, Abigail will come to possess greater and greater influence in Salem. Clearly, only a flawed society could grant power to such a person.

ACT I • SCENE 3

Summary

John Proctor, a well-respected farmer, arrives to fetch his servant, Mary, and to see what "mischief" is brewing. Mary is sent home and Mercy leaves with her. Abigail then confides in Proctor, telling him that the town's suspicions of witchcraft are "posh" and that the girls have only been dancing. Proctor is amused, then concerned as Abigail declares her love for him.

Several months ago, as a servant in Proctor's home, Abigail had become Proctor's mistress. Elizabeth, however, had found out and fired her. Proctor tells Abigail firmly that their affair is over. Abigail is first unbelieving, then tearful, then angry. She turns her anger on Elizabeth, calling her cold and sickly, until Proctor loses his temper.

Abigail again appeals to Proctor to change his mind, claiming that he taught her "what pretense Salem was" and what hypocrites the Puritan townspeople were. Her pleas come to a sudden end as a psalm rises from below, and Betty claps her hands to her ears and begins to whine.

The scene ends with the entry of Parris.

Commentary

As Miller states in his background notes, John Proctor, with his quiet confidence, even temper and good sense, has little patience for fools and hypocrites. However, because of his affair with Abigail, he has come to regard himself as a kind of fraud. Seducing a 17-year-old girl is a sin, not only against

Salem's moral laws, but against his personal sense of honor. By keeping it a secret, Proctor, who despises pretense, has become a hypocrite.

Proctor is a man torn between his physical passions and his inner convictions. Abigail is his temptress: beautiful and frankly wanton, she has tried to seduce him away from Elizabeth, his virtuous but distant wife. Even though Proctor has ended his affair with Abigail, he still sometimes walks to her house at night to look longingly up at her window. Just as Abigail has tempted Proctor, so she will seduce all the Salemites to turn their backs on the truth and indulge themselves in an orgy of hysterical lies and hallucinations, sensational confessions, open greed and ruthless vengeance.

Proctor's sin will prove impossible to leave behind. In this scene, Abigail makes Proctor a witness to the truth by telling him that, far from practising witchcraft, she and her friends were simply frolicking in the woods. This admission of the truth will later place Proctor in a terrible dilemma: he will not be able to give his testimony without confessing to adultery.

Abigail also shows that her love for Proctor cannot be easily dismissed. Abigail's love is motivated by strong and dangerous passions. Those passions will later result in the arrest and trial of Proctor, his wife and many others.

ACT I • SCENE 4

Summary

Parris runs into the room when he hears his daughter's cries. He is followed by the Putnams, Rebecca Nurse and Giles Corey. Rebecca, a respected, elderly woman, gently examines Betty, who immediately calms down. Rebecca states that Betty is simply in her "silly season," and will soon snap out of her hysteria. Rebecca and Proctor criticize Parris for summoning Reverend Hale, a witch-hunter, without consulting anyone else.

Parris and the Putnams accuse Proctor of poor church attendance. In turn, Proctor accuses Parris of being a hell-and-damnation preacher, worried more about his salary, firewood and the deed to his house than about the welfare of his congregation. Giles Corey, an irascible old man, enters the argument on Proctor's side. Parris accuses Proctor of leading a party against himself and "all authority" and Proctor responds that he would like to join such a party. Rebecca tries to make peace between the men, but fails.

Proctor invites Giles Corey to help him drag home some lumber from land recently purchased from Rebecca and her husband. Putnam claims rightful ownership of this land, through his grandfather's will. Proctor and Corey deny Putnam's claim, and Putnam threatens to sue.

As Proctor and Corey are about to leave, the Reverend Hale arrives.

Commentary

This scene clearly shows some of the many boundary disputes, political quibbles, power struggles and petty arguments that exploded in the witch hunts. Proctor, Putnam and Parris disagree on basic matters of church policy. Proctor does not believe that Parris should have sent for Hale without the consent of the congregation. He also questions Parris' right to a deed to the meeting-house and criticizes his preoccupation with hellfire and damnation. The Putnams are involved in disputes over land boundaries with the Proctors and the Nurses. Reverend Parris feels cheated because he is expected to supply his own firewood. And Giles Corey has been involved in six law suits that year alone.

As Miller's notes point out, many accusations of witchcraft were aimed by men such as Putnam at real or imagined enemies out of vengeance or land-greed. The real Putnam had many motives for his malice. His personal candidate for minister had been rejected by the community and his family had been involved in a series of land disputes. The real Nurses were involved in a break-away community that challenged Salem's authority and the Putnams' influence. Not surprisingly, two Putnams signed the first complaint against Rebecca Nurse.

Scene 4 also shows that John Proctor is not a man who blindly accepts authority. As religious leader of the community, Parris insists on total obedience: "It is not for you to say what is good for you to hear!" Proctor rejects this statement, in the name of personal freedom: "I may speak my heart, I think!" Parris then furiously accuses Proctor of leading a faction against him. Although Proctor denies knowledge of such a faction, he states that he would join it if he did. As he tells Rebecca, "I like not the smell of this 'authority.'"

Proctor, then, must respect rules before he obeys them. He considers his own sense of right and wrong more important than the laws of institutions. Significantly, Parris accuses Proctor of speaking like a Quaker, who have always put their individual consciences before established authority.

Scene 4 also introduces us to Rebecca Nurse. Rebecca is the model of virtue and wisdom against whom all the characters in the play can be measured. She is gentle, temperate and peace-loving, and she is respected by almost everyone in the community. In this scene, she calms the hysterical Betty and tries to patch up the quarrel between Parris and Proctor. Her statement that the girls are simply in their silly seasons is sensible and accurate, unlike the superstitions and extreme reactions of Parris and the Putnams. The fact that Rebecca is later tried and executed as a witch shows the depth of absurdity and chaos into which Salem will plunge.

ACT I • SCENE 5

Summary

Reverend Hale, an expert on witches, arrives to examine Betty. He listens to the accounts of Parris and the Putnams and prepares eagerly to do battle with the Devil for Betty's soul. John Proctor, who knows that witchcraft is not involved, leaves the room in disgust. He is soon followed by Rebecca Nurse, who does not wish to see Betty hurt.

When Betty doesn't respond, Hale questions Abigail and Parris about the dancing in the woods. Under Hale's prompting, Abigail grows increasingly hysterical and finally accuses Tituba of tempting her into various forms of evil, including the drinking of blood. Tituba is sent for and threatened with hanging unless she admits to witchcraft. Frightened for her life, Tituba falls to her knees and confesses that she has worked for the Devil, along with other witches.

Hale makes it clear to the terrified Tituba that she can save herself by identifying the "Devil's agents" in the village. Under Hale's and Putnam's prompting, she claims to have seen two unpopular women in the Devil's company. Abigail, inspired by the general hysteria, takes up the cry and names other women that she has seen with the Devil.

Betty then rises feverishly from the bed and joins Abigail in calling out names. Hale and Parris give thanks to God that the spell is broken. Putnam leaves to fetch the marshal to arrest the women named by the girls, while Abigail and Betty continue to cry out names.

Commentary

According to Miller's notes, Reverend Hale cannot be judged too harshly for his belief in witchcraft, even though he is an intellectual. Even today, we believe in a world divided between the forces of good and the forces of evil. We are still happy to view our enemies as the Devil's allies, and to ignore the facts that get in the way of this view. Today, however, ideas of good and evil are more likely to take a directly political form. Just as many religions have called their enemies witches, modern capitalists and communists consider their own beliefs holy and condemn each another as demons.

Reverend Hale is not an evil man. He genuinely believes that the Devil exists and can be fought with the knowledge in his books. His ideals are noble: he wants to purge Salem of evil and return it, cleansed, to the hands of God.

However, in his enthusiasm, Hale puts words into the mouths of Abigail, Tituba and Betty. While questioning them, he prods them to tell him what he wants to hear. He plants details in their minds, like the frog in the soup, and makes it clear that they will be forgiven everything if they name other witches. As a result, he sets into motion events that will lead to the hanging of many innocent people. Hale eventually comes to a horrified understanding of what he has done, though it is too late to do any good.

In fairness to Hale, he could not have foreseen the malice and fanaticism of Abigail Williams. When Hale presses Tituba for names, she provides them reluctantly to save her own life. Abigail, however, volunteers her names willingly and out of spite. She has many grudges against the women of Salem, whom she considers cold, hypocritical gossips. Now she sees a way to become respected and powerful in the community. At the same time, she will take her revenge, particularly against Elizabeth Proctor, who fired her, tarnished her reputation and stole John Proctor back from her.

At this point, John Proctor believes that he can simply turn his back and live his own life, untouched by events that shape society. Unlike Rebecca, who implies that the witch hunt is evil, Proctor refuses to take a stand: "I never spoke on witches one way or the other." He leaves so that he does not have to commit himself, unaware that he is soon to be a part of the witch hunt events.

John Proctor has declared himself against authority, and Hale's books are "weighted with authority." Because the Puritan Church views its enemies as Satan's allies, it is inevitable that Proctor, because of his insistence for personal freedom, will ultimately be accused of witchcraft. In a time of crisis, no one can wash his hands of responsibility.

ACT II • SCENE 1

Summary

Act II takes place eight days later. John Proctor enters his home after working all day in the fields. Elizabeth, his wife, puts their children to bed and serves him dinner. As the couple discuss the farm and the meal, relations between them appear strained and distant.

Elizabeth tells Proctor that their servant, Mary Warren, has gone to Salem against his orders. Mary has become an official of the newly-created court. Fourteen people have been imprisoned on the testimony of Abigail and her friends and will be hanged unless they confess. Judges have come from Boston, including the Deputy Governor of Massachusetts. Abigail has become extremely powerful and is revered by the townspeople as though she were a saint.

Elizabeth wants Proctor to go to Salem right away and tell the constable of Abigail's statement that the dancing in the woods had nothing to do with witchcraft. Proctor hesitates, because he does not believe that, without other witnesses, his word would be taken against Abigail's. Elizabeth becomes upset, because she had not known that Proctor was alone with Abigail when she told him about the dancing. Elizabeth believes that Proctor won't go to Salem because he still loves Abigail and wants to shield her. Proctor accuses Elizabeth of being cold, hard and unforgiving, and regrets ever having confessed his affair with Abigail.

The scene ends as Mary Warren enters.

Commentary

Unlike Parris' house, with its atmosphere of fear, hypocrisy and superstition, the Proctors' home is orderly and calm. As the scene begins, a portrait of perfect domestic harmony is painted. Proctor returns from the fields to find dinner cooking over a warm fire and his wife upstairs singing gently to the children. This harmony and stability will soon be plunged into chaos by the witch hunt.

Yet, already in the Proctor household, there are signs of trouble. Proctor is late, and hasn't told Elizabeth his whereabouts. Elizabeth's soup is not salty enough. She has forgotten to pour her husband's cider, and she has neglected to pick wild flowers to brighten the house. When Proctor kisses her, she doesn't kiss him back. And she has been unable to prevent her own servant from going to Salem. Clearly, Elizabeth is not all a frontier wife should be.

This scene establishes the relationship between Proctor and Elizabeth and shows how each must grow to attain a better understanding of one another and themselves. Elizabeth has been unable to completely forgive Proctor for his affair with Abigail. She is quick to misinterpret his reluctance to denounce Abigail as an attempt to protect the girl. She is also cold to him when he tries to express affection. As Proctor says, Elizabeth must "learn charity" and "look to her own improvement" before judging her husband. She must come to see the part she has played in driving Proctor into Abigail's arms.

For his part, Proctor must learn to accept responsibility for the results of his actions. His adulterous seduction of a 17-year-old girl has already had serious consequences. Indirectly, Proctor has set in motion the events that have led to the witch hunt. He has stirred up strong passions in Abigail, taught her to despise the hypocrisy of the town, and subjected her to gossip from women whom she would later vengefully accuse of witchcraft. Indeed, the entire dancing episode has arisen from Abigail's desire to hex Elizabeth so that she could have Proctor to herself. Yet Proctor steadfastly maintains that his affair with Abigail is over and forgotten, and has done no real harm.

Proctor must also accept responsibility for the welfare of his society. He is afraid to call Abigail a liar because he suspects that, in order to discredit her, he might have to publicly confess to adultery and lechery. With 14 people already in prison, there is not a moment to lose. Yet, despite his wife's anxious pleading, Proctor is unwilling to commit himself to a course of action. Instead, he will only agree to "think on it" while Abigail's power over the town grows stronger.

ACT II • SCENE 2

Summary

Mary Warren returns, and is scolded by Proctor for neglecting her duties. She presents Elizabeth with a doll she has made and tells them about her day in court. Thirty-nine women have now been arrested, and Goody Osburn, a drunken halfwit, is to be hung.

Mary tells how she herself has confronted Sarah Good, a homeless beggar, with accusations that are clearly absurd. Sarah then confessed to save herself from hanging. Mary also reveals that someone has accused Elizabeth of witchcraft, though the accusation has been dismissed. Carried away by her power as a court official, Mary refuses to take orders from the Proctors and goes off to bed in a huff.

Elizabeth believes that Abigail wants her dead and is behind the accusations against her. Proctor reluctantly agrees and decides to tell the constable that Abigail is lying. Elizabeth also wants Proctor to make it clear to Abigail that he will not marry her if Elizabeth is killed.

Proctor angrily insists that he never gave Abigail any cause to think he'd marry her. Elizabeth replies that Proctor, by sleeping with Abigail, gave her an unspoken promise of love. Moreover, Abigail "has an arrow in you yet, John Proctor, and you know it well."

The scene ends with the arrival of Reverend Hale.

Commentary

Mary Warren's new position as an official of the court shows how the witch hunt has turned the social order of Salem upside down. Mary, an ignorant servant girl, has just come from dinner with four judges and the Deputy Governor. In the Proctor home, she gives orders instead of taking them, and hints that only her testimony stands between Elizabeth and prison. In the same way, Abigail, who is cruel, lying and wanton, is being treated like a saint, while virtuous women like Elizabeth are accused of Devil-worship.

Mary Warren also brings the first news of the court proceedings. Clearly, justice has been placed in the hands of foolish, hysterical girls. Mary's own accusations against the beggar, Sarah Good, are based on the fact that she once became ill shortly after turning Sarah away from the door. This superstitious nonsense is called "hard proof" by the judges, and is enough to condemn Sarah if she doesn't confess.

With his wife accused, Proctor has no choice but to act. On Elizabeth's urging, he agrees to denounce Abigail and to tell her to her face that he despises her. However, he still refuses to admit that, by making love to Abigail, he has led her to believe that she had something to gain by Elizabeth's death. Although Proctor reluctantly agrees to confront Abigail, he is angry at Elizabeth for dragging up the past and forcing him to become involved.

ACT II • SCENE 3

Summary

Reverend Hale arrives, startling Proctor and Elizabeth. Hale no longer seems as sure of himself as he was. He tells the Proctors that he is visiting several households without the court's authority so that he can get to know the characters of those who are accused of witchcraft. He has just been visiting Rebecca Nurse who, like Elizabeth, has been "somewhat mentioned" in the court.

Hale asks Proctor why he is so often absent from church on the Sabbath. Proctor first answers that Elizabeth has been ill. He then admits that he has stayed away out of disgust at Reverend Parris' materialistic greed for such items as golden candlesticks. Proctor has also refused to let Parris baptize his third child because "I see no light of God in that man." Hale tells Proctor that the church, not the individual, decides who has the light of God in him.

Proctor mentions that he actually built the church, along with Francis Nurse. Hale decides to test Proctor by asking him to name the ten commandments. Proctor, much to his dismay, forgets the commandment against adultery.

On Elizabeth's urging, Proctor reluctantly reports Abigail's statement that Betty's illness had nothing to do with witchcraft. Hale is shocked, and tells Proctor that many women have confessed outright to Devil-worship. Proctor points out that people will swear to anything before they'll hang, and adds that he himself is reluctant to tell the truth in a court that shows such poor judgment. Hale is impressed with these arguments. Clearly, he is beginning to doubt the validity of the court proceedings. He warns the Proctors to attend church and baptize their third child, then prepares to leave.

The scene ends with the entrance of Giles Corey and Francis Nurse.

Commentary

In this scene, John Proctor is presented as an individual who refuses to comply with a corrupt authority. Proctor sees Reverend Parris as greedy, materialistic and hypocritical. He refuses to support Parris by attending his services and prefers to break the Sabbath and leave his child unbaptized. It is not enough for him that the church says Parris is holy: Proctor makes his own decisions and sticks by them.

Despite his beliefs, however, Proctor has never done anything to improve the situation in his church. He has always shied away from confrontation by avoiding Parris and limiting his life to his farm. Even now, Proctor has to be prompted by Elizabeth before he tells Hale that Abigail has been lying. He also has no desire to tell his story in court. Proctor is a man who knows what is right but is unwilling to endanger himself to enforce his beliefs.

If Proctor has been too slow to become involved, Hale has been too hasty. Hale also thought he knew what was right, and he believed in the authority of the church above all else. Now he is not so sure. At first the girls had only accused drunks and beggars, but now they have started denouncing respectable, God-fearing women.

Because Hale has begun to doubt the value of the trials, he has decided to investigate on his own, "without the court's authority." Hale is no fool. He knows that people will confess to anything rather than hang, and he is deeply troubled when Proctor tells him of Abigail's deception. He is beginning to suspect that, in his zeal, he may have convicted innocent people.

In their different ways, then, Proctor and Hale are both grappling with their consciences and struggling to come to terms with the combined authority of church and state. Proctor is slowly realizing that he cannot hide on his farm but must directly confront established authority and force it to accept the truth. Hale is gradually growing aware of a need to choose between following his own conscience or continuing to blindly serve a corrupt institution.

ACT II • SCENE 4

Summary

Giles Corey and Francis Nurse arrive to report that their wives have been arrested and taken to prison. Rebecca has been accused of magically killing the Putnams' babies and Martha Corey has been accused of killing the pigs of a man with a grudge against her.

Reverend Hale is surprised and disturbed by the news, and tells Francis that "if Rebecca Nurse be tainted, then nothing's left to stop the whole green world from burning." He assures Francis that Rebecca will be set free, and pleads desperately for the need to fight the Devil's presence in Salem. Hale reminds the others that the guilty can appear completely innocent: "until an hour before the Devil fell, God thought him beautiful in heaven."

The scene ends with the arrival of the marshal and constable.

Commentary

The witch hunt in Salem is now completely out of control. As her husband claims, Rebecca Nurse is "the very brick and mortar of the church." Martha Corey is also a devout, respected Puritan. They have been accused by petty, vengeful and superstitious neighbors and are now at the mercy of a deluded court.

Although Reverend Hale continues to speak for the church, his faith is clearly crumbling. He promises that Rebecca Nurse will be freed, but he is not really sure. Although he is aware of the pain that Francis and Giles are suffering, he feels forced to defend the idea that the Devil is alive in Salem and is hiding in apparently innocent women. Yet, even as he argues this, he seems to be pleading for the men's forgiveness.

ACT II • SCENE 5

Summary

Constable Cheever and Marshal Herrick arrive to arrest Elizabeth. This is their 16th arrest of the night. Abigail Williams has accused Elizabeth of attempted murder by witchcraft. Cheever finds Mary Warren's poppet (rag doll) with a needle stuck in its stomach. Earlier that evening, Abigail had fainted, screaming, and a two-inch needle was found buried in her belly.

Proctor sends for Mary Warren, who admits that the poppet is her own. She had been sewing it in court that day and had stuck the needle in it herself, with Abigail watching. Hale then warns Mary that she is charging Abigail with trying to kill Elizabeth.

Cheever still insists on arresting Elizabeth. Proctor, enraged, damns the court and tries to tear up the warrant. Proctor accuses Parris and Abigail of plotting to destroy Elizabeth. He cries out that "the little crazy children are jangling the keys of the kingdom, and common vengeance writes the law!" When Hale refuses to intervene, Proctor calls him a Pontius Pilate, washing his hands of innocent blood.

Elizabeth consents to go to prison, and she is taken outside and chained. Proctor follows, swearing that he will free her. Herrick and Cheever excuse themselves, saying that they are only following orders.

Proctor refuses to be comforted by Hale and calls him a moral coward. Hale responds that there must be more behind the trouble in Salem than the vengeance of one little girl. Before he leaves, Hale asks Proctor to "think on cause" and to find the source of the evil. Proctor is struck by Hale's words, and asks Francis and Giles to leave him.

As the scene ends, Proctor is left alone on the stage with Mary Warren.

Commentary

Throughout the course of this scene, it becomes known to everyone that Elizabeth has been framed. Clearly, corrupt laws are being used to persecute innocent victims. As Proctor claims, the social order has been destroyed and placed in the hands of foolish, irresponsible and vengeful children.

The characters react to this crisis in a number of different ways. Francis Nurse and Giles Corey stand by, helpless and confused, powerless against the nine men that wait outside to take Elizabeth away. Cheever and Herrick refuse to take personal responsibility for their actions. Herrick states that the "law binds me . . . I cannot budge." Like a Nazi in a concentration camp, he is just following orders.

Reverend Hale, who believes Elizabeth innocent, turns away and refuses to intervene, unwilling to take a stand against the authority of the church. Like Pontius Pilate, he prefers to wash his hands of guilt in the hope that events will turn out for the best. Until recently, Proctor has also washed his hands of personal responsibility. Now, with his wife torn from him, he finally commits himself to fighting the corruption that has invaded Salem. He will "fall like an ocean on that court" to save Elizabeth's life.

Proctor is stung, however, by Hale's claim that some greater sin than Abigail's desire for revenge must be the source of so much evil. Proctor suddenly realizes that his seduction of Abigail has been a primary cause of the events of the past few days. To the Puritans, adultery, or lechery, was a terrible sin. Even today, the seduction of a minor by an adult is considered rape. By seducing Abigail and then rejecting her, Proctor has made Abigail hate Elizabeth. By causing Abigail to fall in love with him, Proctor has prepared the way for the destruction of his family. And, to avoid publicly confessing his sin, he has delayed in denouncing Abigail until it is too late.

This scene also contrasts the behavior of Elizabeth and Abigail. We see how fanatical Abigail has become when we hear how she has driven a two-inch needle into her own belly to trap Elizabeth. In contrast, Elizabeth is calm under pressure and concerned for others. Though frightened for her life, she makes sure that her family will be cared for in her absence and that bread will be baked for the children the next day. She is led away to her chains with dignity, and never indulges in the feverish hysterics that are typical of Abigail.

ACT II • SCENE 6

Summary

Proctor and Mary Warren are left alone in the house. Mary tries to reassure Proctor that Elizabeth will be all right. Proctor orders her to go with him and tell the court how she herself stuck the needle into the poppet. Mary tells Proctor that Abigail will kill her and denounce him as a lecher.

Proctor hesitates. Then, hating himself, he declares, "Good . . . We will slide together into our pit." When Mary insists that she cannot testify, Proctor grabs her by the throat.

As the act ends, Mary sobs in terror while Proctor rails at the night, crying that "the wind, God's icy wind, will blow!"

Commentary

If Proctor denounces Abigail as a liar to save Elizabeth, Abigail will accuse him of lechery. Proctor quickly realizes that, to prove him a lecher, Abigail will have to confess to harlotry. As a harlot, Abigail's power will truly be broken, and Elizabeth will go free.

Mary Warren is terrified of Abigail and does not want to testify against her. However, in this scene, she becomes more terrified of Proctor. Rage and grief have nearly driven Proctor out of his mind. Earlier, he had tried to remain apart from the madness that swept through Salem. Now he finds that it has engulfed his life and destroyed his home.

ACT III • SCENE 1

Summary

Act III takes place in the vestry of the Salem prayer house, which is now the anteroom of the court. Offstage, in the courtroom, Martha Corey is being questioned. Her husband, Giles, tries to present new evidence, and is dragged into the vestry by Marshal Herrick.

Corey and Herrick are joined by Francis Nurse, Reverend Hale, Reverend Parris, Constable Cheever, Judge Hathorne, and Deputy Governor Danforth, who is in charge of the court. Hathorne is decribed as a "bitter, remorseless Salem judge." Danforth is described as a grave man "with an exact loyalty to his position and his cause."

Corey and Nurse have been waiting three days to present their evidence. Meanwhile, Rebecca and Elizabeth have already been condemned. Nurse tells Danforth that they have proof that the girls are lying. Danforth is shocked, and tells Nurse that he has already signed nearly 400 arrest warrants and condemned 72 people to hang on the girls' testimony.

Proctor enters with Mary Warren and is accused by Parris of trying to overthrow the court. With Proctor's coaxing, Mary admits that she has never seen any spirits and that she and the other girls have been pretending. Danforth questions Proctor about his motives in presenting this evidence. Proctor replies that he just wants to free his wife.

Danforth hears complaints from Parris and Cheever that Proctor has damned the court, seldom attends church and plows on Sunday. He then tells Proctor that Elizabeth may be pregnant, in which case she will be kept alive for a year. He asks Proctor to drop his evidence, since Elizabeth's life is not threatened. Proctor, after hesitating, refuses, because his friends' wives are also accused.

Proctor presents a petition that 91 upstanding farmers have signed praising the good characters of Elizabeth, Rebecca and Martha. Parris calls the petition an attempt to overthrow the court. Hale responds by asking, "Is every defense an attack upon the court?" Parris persuades Danforth to have the 91 farmers arrested for examination. Francis Nurse is horrified by this. When he collected the names, he promised those who signed that no harm would come to them.

Proctor next presents Giles Corey's deposition charging Putnam with falsely accusing a neighbor of witchcraft to seize his property. Putnam is sent for and denies the charge. Corey has a witness who heard Putnam announce his intention; however, if he gives the witness' name, the man will be arrested. Because he will not reveal his witness' name, Corey is arrested for contempt of court. When Hale objects, Danforth absurdly states that, "no uncorrupted man may fear this court."

Scene 1 ends as Proctor prepares to present the testimony of Mary Warren.

Commentary

Scene 1 shows the full horror and absurdity of a court in which the wild lies and hysterical ravings of children have so far caused 400 arrests and 72 death sentences. The house of prayer has been corrupted, and justice has been turned completely upside down. As Danforth states, "The entire contention of the state in these trials is that the voice of Heaven is speaking through the children." Yet we know that the children, led by Abigail, are vicious and deceitful, and that their victims are honest and virtuous.

Danforth has had no difficulty believing that spirits fly daily through his court slashing at victims with daggers. Nonetheless, when faced with a rational explanation of the girls' behavior, he immediately dismisses it as a fantastic deceit. When Mary Warren admits that the girls have been pretending, he is amazed that she has the nerve to come to him with such a lie.

Clearly, the court, under Danforth, is in the midst of a reign of terror. As Hale says, "There is a prodigious fear of this court in the country." Innocent people have been seized from their homes throughout Massachusetts. Some, like Putnams' neighbor, are victims of their accusers' lust for property. Others, like Elizabeth, have been accused out of jealousy and vengeance. Still others, like the 91 farmers who signed the petition, might be arrested simply because they have dared to suggest that the court is mistaken.

The judges of the court are harsh, proud men who will not tolerate any opposition. As Hale points out, any defense is seen as an attack, and any suggestion that the court could be mistaken is seen as an attempt to overthrow its authority. Although the purpose of a court of law is to find out the truth, this court spreads only fantastic lies. Those who attempt to tell the truth are arrested as witches, then forced into false confessions.

In its refusal to tolerate opposition and its insistence that witnesses incriminate other people by naming names, the Salem court is identical to the McCarthy hearings of the early 1950s. In those hearings, all those who refused to co-operate with the court by providing the names of suspected communists were themselves considered communists. When Danforth states that "a person is either with this court or . . . against it, there be no road between," he echoes McCarthy's belief that those who criticized his hearings could only be communists.

Until recently, John Proctor has tried desperately to find a middle ground, neither for nor against the court. Now he has begun to realize that Danforth is right. There is "no road between." By his silence, Proctor has supported the court. When he first decided to break his silence and fight its authority, he wanted only to save his wife. In this scene, Proctor takes his commitment one step further. Danforth tells him that Elizabeth's life will be spared for at least a year. He invites Proctor to take back his evidence before he has placed his own life in danger. Proctor is tempted to compromise, but refuses, because his evidence might also save the wives of his friends. He has begun to place the common good beyond his individual concerns, and to commit himself to a purpose larger than himself.

At this stage, however, Proctor still has a naive belief in the justice of the court. He tells Mary Warren to remember the words of the angel Raphael: "Do that which is good, and no harm shall come to you." He believes that the court will welcome the truth and willingly reserve its decisions. Proctor has no idea that, by insisting on truth and reason in the midst of deceit and hysteria, he is signing his own death warrant.

ACT III • SCENE 2

Summary

Proctor prepares to present Mary Warren's deposition that the girls have been lying. Hale interrupts and begs Danforth to let Proctor appear with a lawyer. Hale has signed 72 death warrants and wants to make absolutely sure that the girls are not lying. Danforth explains to him that a lawyer could not possibly do any good. Witchcraft is an invisible crime that only the witch and the victim can witness. Since the witch will not accuse herself, the victim's testimony must always be believed.

Mary tells Danforth that she has never seen Satan or any other spirit. She has been lying, even though she knew people would hang by her evidence. Danforth questions her and, when she sticks to her story, tells her that she will be imprisoned for perjury.

Abigail, Betty, Mercy and Susanna are shown into the vestry and faced with Mary's testimony. Abigail denies that she and the girls have been lying. Danforth tells Abigail that she is accused of framing Elizabeth Proctor. Mary has admitted to sticking the needle into the poppet herself, in Abigail's presence. Again, Abigail denies Mary's testimony.

Proctor tells Danforth that Abigail is fully capable of murder, and that she is no innocent child. She has recently been disciplined twice for laughing in prayers. Furthermore, she has led the girls to dance naked in the woods. Parris reluctantly agrees that he caught the girls dancing, though fully dressed. Danforth is disturbed by this evidence, and begins to lose faith in Abigail.

Mary tells Hathorne that she has only pretended to faint, choke and turn cold in court. Hathorne asks her to faint for them now as a demonstration. Mary tries to put herself in the right frame of mind, but is unable to do so. She finally admits that, although she hasn't actually seen spirits, she did think she saw them. She has been deluded by the other girls' screaming and by the general hysteria of the court.

Danforth asks Abigail if she, too, could have been deluded into thinking she saw spirits where none existed. Abigail indignantly rejects these suspicions, and calls them a poor reward for all she has suffered in the name of God. She warns Danforth that he, himself, is not immune from Satan's power.

The scene ends as Abigail suddenly begins to shiver and claim that Mary is witching her.

Commentary

Once again, we see the absurd and deadly logic of the court. As Parris states, the court exists "precisely to discover what no one has ever seen." Because witchcraft is an invisible crime, there can be no witnesses. And because the witch will naturally lie to defend herself, her word can never be taken. Therefore, the accuser must always be right, and the accused must always be guilty. Danforth sees no flaw in this perversion of justice. He willingly suspends due process of law, and never doubts his ability to make accurate judgments.

Throughout this scene, Mary's testimony is being weighed against Abigail's. Certainly, Mary's story of deluded girls is much more believable than Abigail's mad tales of witches, spirits and fantastic attacks on her body. Yet Danforth would rather believe Abigail's far-fetched lies than believe that he has been wrong. If Mary's story is true, then he has commited 72 innocent people to their deaths.

Unfortunately, Mary is not as convincing when telling the truth as Abigail is when lying. Mary is a timid girl with little charm or intelligence. Abigail is a beautiful girl and a brilliant liar. Mary lacks the imagination to pretend to faint when not stirred up by the others. Abigail has no such problem. She is a natural actress. Danforth is thoroughly captivated by Abigail. He is also a little frightened of her. He backs off quickly when she challenges his power by reminding him that he is not immune from the accusation of witchcraft.

Unlike Danforth and Hathorne, Hale feels severe doubts about the guilt of the people he has helped to convict. Hale no longer believes blindly in the authority of the church. He has signed 72 death warrants, including that of Rebecca Nurse, and his "hand shakes yet as with a wound." An intelligent man, he has seen the absurdity of the court's position and is now trying to inject some reason into the proceedings.

Hale points out to Danforth that not everyone who is accused is necessarily guilty and that not everyone who tries to defend himself is attacking the court's authority. He begs Danforth to let Proctor find a lawyer to present Mary Warren's testimony, because "in all justice, sir, a claim so weighty cannot be argued by a farmer." Although Hale accepts Danforth's refusal, he has moved closer to the point when he will finally listen to his conscience and break away from the court.

ACT III • SCENE 3

Summary

Confronted with Mary's testimony, Abigail suddenly begins to shiver with fear. She accuses Mary of menacing her by sending out her spirit in the form of a cold shadow. Mercy and Susanna follow Abigail's lead and also begin to shiver. Danforth is completely taken in and orders Mary to stop. Mary, terrified, starts to run and is caught by Proctor.

As Abigail prays, Proctor leaps toward her. Dragging her to her feet by the hair, he calls her a whore and asks her how she dares call Heaven. He tells the court that he is a lecher, and abandons his good name. He explains, his voice broken with shame, that Abigail has framed Elizabeth because she "thinks to dance with me on my wife's grave." Elizabeth had fired Abigail as a harlot, and now Abigail is seeking "a whore's vengeance."

Danforth is shocked by the testimony. Despite Abigail's indignant denials, he orders her to remain in the room while Elizabeth is sent for. Danforth asks Proctor if Elizabeth is honest, and he replies that she is incapable of lying. Danforth then states that, if Elizabeth claims to have fired Abigail for harlotry, Abigail will be totally discredited. He orders Abigail and Proctor to turn their backs and tells Elizabeth to enter.

The scene ends with the entry of Elizabeth.

Commentary

After Abigail terrifies Mary into silence, Proctor finally sees that he can only stop her through the sacrifice of his good name. Proctor has dreaded this sacrifice, and done everything in his power to prevent or postpone it. As he calls Abigail a whore and himself a lecher, his world crumbles around him. The damage to his reputation can never be repaired. Right away, he loses the esteem of his valued friend, Francis Nurse.

Yet, if this is a moment of great shame for Proctor, it is also a moment of great heroism. Proctor has sacrificed what means most to him, his honor, so his wife and the wives of his friends may live. From this point, there is no turning back for Proctor. Eventually he will regain his honor, but only at the cost of his life.

ACT III • SCENE 4

Summary

Danforth summons Elizabeth and orders her not to look at her husband. He asks her why she dismissed Abigail as her servant. Elizabeth doesn't know what to say, and repeats that her husband is a good man. Under Danforth's questioning, she admits only that, when she was ill, she had thought Abigail was stealing Proctor from her.

Danforth asks Elizabeth directly whether Proctor has ever committed the crime of lechery. Elizabeth stalls and is unable to answer. Danforth then asks her if her husband *is* a lecher, to which she faintly replies, "No, sir." Proctor cries out to Elizabeth that he has confessed to the crime, and Elizabeth is led in tears from the room.

Hale believes Proctor, and claims that Elizabeth has only lied to protect her husband. He tells Danforth that he can no longer refuse to listen to his conscience. Danforth ignores Hale. Elizabeth's testimony has convinced him that Abigail is innocent and that Proctor is a liar.

The scene ends as Abigail enters another hysterical trance.

Commentary

In his eagerness to praise Elizabeth to the court, Proctor has presented her as a woman who cannot lie. He believes this to be true. As we have seen in Act II, Elizabeth has tried many times to force her husband to be honest with himself. But Proctor underestimates Elizabeth's love for him. To save her husband's honor, she is prepared to distort the truth.

Technically, Elizabeth does not really lie. When Danforth asks him if Proctor has ever committed lechery, she simply doesn't answer. When, however, he asks if Proctor *is* a lecher, she can truthfully answer no. The fact that Proctor has come to the court proves that Abigail no longer has any claim on his heart; therefore he is no longer guilty, even in his mind, of adultery.

Nonetheless, Elizabeth does not tell the whole truth, and the truth she does tell is distorted. It is a central irony of the play that, by sacrificing her uncompromising honesty out of love for her husband, Elizabeth condemns him as a liar and proves Abigail's innocence. Miller's message is clear: total honesty and total integrity are the only tools that can combat evil.

In this scene, the Reverend Hale finally takes his stand against the injustice of the court. He clearly states his belief in Proctor's testimony and his distrust of Abigail. He can no longer shut his conscience to the fact that "private vengeance is working through this testimony." However, Hale's attempts to intervene prove useless. He has no power to save lives, only to condemn them.

ACT III • SCENE 5

Summary

As Hale accuses her of lying, Abigail screams out with fear and points, terrified, to the ceiling. The other girls follow suit. Abigail begins to speak to an invisible yellow bird that waits on the roofbeam to tear her face. She claims that the bird is Mary Warren, who has changed her shape to attack her.

As Proctor and Mary protest, Abigail and the girls become glassy-eyed and begin to mimic everything Mary says. Danforth is convinced by the performance and demands that Mary draw back her spirit from the girls. Despite protests from Proctor and Hale, Danforth accuses Mary of reversing her testimony at Satan's bidding. Mary, terrified, panics and begins to scream. She then turns on Proctor, shrieking madly, and calls him the Devil's man.

In hysterics, Mary tells Danforth that Proctor has come to her every day and night to make her sign the Devil's book. She claims that he has threatened to murder her unless she helped him overthrow the court. Mary runs to Abigail, and falls sobbing into her arms.

Danforth is completely deluded by Mary's mad accusations and calls Proctor the anti-Christ, "befouled with Hell." He orders Proctor to confess his "black allegiance." Proctor is dumfounded and furious. He shouts that God is dead, and that he and Danforth will burn together for concealing the truth.

Danforth orders the marshal to take Proctor and Corey to prison. Hale denounces the court's proceedings and leaves the room. He slams the door behind him as Danforth furiously calls him back.

Commentary

Once again, Abigail proves herself a creative liar and a brilliant actress. The power of her performance reduces the solemn Deputy Governor Danforth to near-hysteria, and terrifies Hathorne and Parris. Mary is completely destroyed by the performance, and driven over the edge into temporary madness. Her will-power crumbles before the onslaught of Danforth, Abigail and Parris, and she can no longer recall the angel Raphael's instruction to do only what is good. Indeed, she no longer knows what is good, and surrenders herself completely to Abigail's influence.

As Proctor is condemned by Danforth, he shouts wildly that God is dead. This is used as further evidence of his pact with Satan; it is actually a statement of despair. According to the Puritans, God controlled all aspects of life on earth. If evil can triumph so easily over virtue, and deceit hold such power over truth, then the world no longer makes sense. If the world makes no sense, then God must no longer be alive. Proctor's words are prophetic for God's power was soon to die in Massachusetts. According to Miller, the witch trials destroyed the theocracy and ended religious power in state manners.

If Proctor no longer believes in God, he certainly believes in Hell. He believes that he has indeed done Satan's work by not denouncing Abigail earlier. Out of fear for his good name, he has delayed in testifying to the truth, and for this he will burn in Hell, along with Danforth and the others. Reverend Hale is deeply impressed with Proctor's speech. Sickened by Proctor's arrest, he finally acts according to his conscience and denounces the court. However, his moral conversion comes too late to save those that he has already condemned.

ACT IV • SCENE 1

Summary
Three months have passed. Summer has turned to autumn, the season of death and decay. In the pre-dawn darkness, a drunken Marshal Herrick is trying to move Sarah Good and Tituba out of their prison cell.

The two women are half-mad and believe they really are witches. Tituba, the West Indian slave, has promised Sarah, a beggar, that the Devil will transform them both into bluebirds and lead them to Barbados. As Tituba explains to Herrick, the Devil "freeze his soul in Massachusetts" but "him be pleasure-man in Barbados."

Tituba becomes convinced that the mooing of a nearby un-milked cow is a sign that the Devil has come for them. At the same time, Hopkins, a guard, announces the arrival of Deputy Governor Danforth. Hopkins and Herrick drag Sarah and Tituba from the cell, as Tituba calls out for the Devil to take her home.

The scene ends with the entry of Danforth and Judge Hathorne.

Commentary
Scene 1 offers a few moments of comic relief to break the almost unbearable dramatic tension that ends Act III. Two foolish and demented women, convinced that they really are witches, expect Satan to arrive at any moment. They look forward eagerly to being turned into bluebirds so they can fly away.

Even this comic portrait, however, is tinged with pathos. The women's madness is a result of ignorance and ill-treatment.

In their dank, squalid cell, they can hardly be blamed for keeping hope alive any way they can.

Tituba, especially, is a pathetic figure, despite her breezy high spirits. She has been locked away among strangers as a result of laws she doesn't understand. In her own land the Devil is honored as the lord of festivals and celebrations. Now she cries out to the Devil to take her home, away from the cold laws and customs of Massachusetts.

Indeed, Barbados was not the only place where the Devil was loved as a figure of festivity and abandon. Throughout the world, dozens of cultures have made room for periods of intense merrymaking in which various demons were honored. For the Puritans, however, such pleasures were sinful, illegal and severely punished.

Herrick's grim drunkenness also injects a serious note into the women's comic ravings. His statement to Tituba that "it's the proper moment to fly into Hell" gives us the first sign that this is the morning on which John Proctor, Rebecca Nurse and others are to be hanged.

ACT IV • SCENE 2

Summary

Deputy Governor Danforth, Judge Hathorne and Constable Cheever arrive at the prison. They learn that Reverend Hale and Reverend Parris have been praying all night with Rebecca Nurse and other condemned prisoners. Danforth is angry at Hale's presence, and sends for Parris.

Hathorne tells Danforth that Parris may be going mad. Cheever explains that Parris has been under a lot of pressure to settle disagreements among farmers concerning the cattle that are roaming wild, abandoned by their imprisoned owners. Parris then enters, "gaunt, frightened, and sweating in his greatcoat."

Parris explains to Danforth that Hale has been urging Rebecca, Martha Corey and others to confess and save their lives. Danforth is pleased, although so far the women have not weakened. Parris then breaks down and admits that Abigail and Mercy Lewis have stolen his savings and run away on a ship. He claims that Abigail has run off because she was frightened by the news of rebellion against the court in nearby Andover.

Parris says that he, too, is frightened that the rebellion is spreading into Salem. That night, his own life had been threatened. So far, only drunkards and outcasts have been executed. However, if Rebecca Nurse, John Proctor and five other respected citizens are hung that morning as scheduled, a riot may break out. Parris begs Danforth to postpone the hangings until at least one of the condemned confesses and proves that all seven are guilty. Danforth refuses, but agrees to do his best to force a confession from one of the prisoners before dawn.

Reverend Hale enters, exhausted, and asks Danforth to pardon the prisoners. Danforth again refuses, stating that "reprieve or pardon must cast doubt upon the guilt of them that died till now." He claims that the prisoners are to die under God's law, which cannot be altered for any reason.

Danforth asks whether Proctor has shown any signs of relenting. Herrick tells him that Proctor is chained to the wall and, except for eating occasionally, shows few signs of life. Danforth decides that Elizabeth, now three months pregnant, may be able to soften Proctor. He sends Herrick to fetch her.

Hale tells Danforth that his merciless justice will force Salem to rebel. Already there are orphans wandering in the streets, abandoned cattle in the roads, rotting crops in the fields and fear in every household. Hale admits that he has been begging the prisoners to confess and save themselves, even though he knows that the accusations are lies. He is acting out of terrible guilt. "Can you not see the blood on my head!!" he cries.

The scene ends with the arrival of Elizabeth Proctor and Herrick.

Commentary

Clearly, the court's reign of terror is on the verge of causing open rebellion. In the months since the witch hunt first began, Salem has been plunged into chaos. Abandoned crops rot in the fields, while the children of prisoners go hungry. Farmers quarrel over the cattle of their arrested neighbors, and all Salemites live in constant fear for their lives. Already there are rumors of rebellion against the court in nearby Andover.

Deputy Governor Danforth refuses to listen to anything that he doesn't want to hear. He avoids discussing Andover at all. Then he tells Parris, against the facts, that the rebellion has been put down. When Parris tells him that Abigail has stolen money and left town, Danforth refuses to call her testimony into question. And when told that the hanging of respected citizens without their confessions will cause a riot in the town, Danforth answers that "I cannot pardon these when twelve are already hanged for the same crime. It is not just." In the name of justice, more innocent people must die.

Yet, even though Danforth is merciless, pompous and blind to the truth, he does at least believe he is right. To Danforth, the letter of the law comes straight from God. As the head of the court, he believes that he has acted with God's authority. God's law has no room for mercy; "an ocean of salt tears could not melt the resolution of the statutes."

To Danforth's credit, he refuses to enforce one law for social outcasts and another for powerful citizens. He is also no coward, and claims that he would "hang ten thousand that dared rise against the law." For both these reasons, Danforth is far superior to Parris. Frightened for his life and robbed of his savings, Parris is finally revealed as a self-serving, whimpering coward. His desire to postpone the hangings of Rebecca and Proctor has nothing to do with concern for their lives. He wants only to protect himself from attacks from angry townspeople. It is fitting that Parris' life savings are stolen by his own niece; it was Parris' greed for gold that first drove Proctor away from church.

If Parris wants the hangings postponed out of fear, Hale wants them postponed out of guilt. Parris wants one of the prisoners to confess so that the others will appear to be guilty. Hale wants the prisoners to confess so that they will live and their blood will not be on his hands.

Reverend Hale is at least honest about his motives. He is also clearly opposed "to do the Devil's work. I come to counsel Christians they should belie themselves." Hale does not, however, seem concerned that, by asking the prisoners to confess, he is asking them to help the court to prevent open rebellion in Salem.

ACT IV • SCENE 3

Summary

Elizabeth is brought into the cell in chains. She is pale and thin, and her clothes are dirty. Hale tells her that Proctor is to hang that morning. He blames himself for Proctor's arrest and asks Elizabeth to convince Proctor to confess and save his life.

In his attempt to persuade Elizabeth, Hale argues eloquently for Proctor's confession. He points to his own role in the witch hunt, and warns her to "cleave to no faith when faith brings blood." Hale claims that no principle is worth the loss of a life, and that "it may well be that God damns a liar less than he that throws his life away for pride." Elizabeth replies quietly that these are the Devil's arguments.

Danforth accuses Elizabeth of lacking all "wifely tenderness." He claims that her stony silence is proof that she has lost her soul to the Devil. Finally Elizabeth agrees to speak with her husband, but does not promise to ask for his confession.

The scene ends with the entry of John Proctor, in chains.

Commentary

In this scene, the various distorted positions of Danforth, Hathorne, Parris and Hale are contrasted against the simple honesty of Elizabeth. In particular, Hale's arguments, though seemingly reasonable and practical, are shown to be corrupt.

For three months, Hale has struggled to find a way of coming to terms with the guilt caused by his part in the witch hunt. Finally he has decided to urge the prisoners to confess to lies and save themselves from hanging. To support their decision, he argues that life is God's most precious gift and must not be thrown away for a principle. He claims that lying may well be a lesser sin than sacrificing one's life out of pride, and tells Elizabeth that no one can claim to truly know God's will.

When Elizabeth calls these the Devil's arguments, she is basing her argument only on her strong personal sense of right and wrong. And indeed, her judgment is accurate. If John Proctor confesses, the court will use that confession to destroy the good names of Rebecca and the others. The court will therefore prevent the possibility of open rebellion and increase its corrupt hold over Salem.

Clearly, throughout this scene, Elizabeth is suffering deeply out of love for Proctor. Danforth, however, sees only a woman who refuses to save her husband's life. His accusations of heartlessness add a bitter taste of irony to Elizabeth's anguish.

ACT IV • SCENE 4

Summary

Proctor enters in chains, led by Herrick. He is bearded and filthy. He seems like another man. He and Elizabeth, who have been apart for three months, stare deeply into one another's eyes. The intensity of the moment overwhelms Hale, who persuades the others to leave.

Left alone together, Proctor and Elizabeth clasp hands and begin, with difficulty, to speak. Elizabeth learns that Proctor has been tortured. She tells him that their sons are safe, but that Giles Corey has been tortured to death. She adds that, although many have confessed, Rebecca, Martha Corey and others have held firm.

Proctor asks Elizabeth how she would feel if he confessed. Although he has so far remained silent out of stubbornness and spite, he claims that he would be dishonest if he were to die like a saint. His lechery has already destroyed his good name and damned his soul; one more lie wouldn't matter. To be killed like a martyr would be a vain pretense. Moreover, as a father, he has a responsibility to free himself and make a living for his children.

Proctor desperately wants Elizabeth to approve his confession. Elizabeth insists that she cannot judge or forgive him. It is his own soul that he is risking. She tells him, however, that whatever he does, she knows he is a good man. In her months in prison, Elizabeth has searched her soul. She knows now that her own insecurity and coldness drove Proctor into Abigail's arms. Proctor denies this confession, in great pain.

The scene ends as Judge Hathorne returns.

Commentary

So far, Proctor has refused to confess to witchcraft out of stubborn pride. Despite torture, he has not wanted "to give a lie to dogs." Now he is planning to confess to save his life. He desperately wants Elizabeth to approve this action. In his heart, however, he knows that it is cowardly.

Clearly, Proctor is not yet being fully honest with himself. Although he does not quite realize that his confession would betray his friends and strengthen the power of the court, he does know that it would be a cowardly act. Eagerly, he asks Elizabeth if Rebecca, Giles or Martha have confessed. As he hears about the courage and integrity of each of his friends, he almost seems disappointed.

Ironically, the arguments that Proctor uses to conceal the truth from himself all support the need for honesty. He claims that if he died like a saint he would be guilty of dishonest vanity. He is not a saint, but an adulterer and a sinner. According to Proctor, a confession of lies is more honest than a proud and undeserving death as a martyr. In this argument, he echoes Hale's statement that "God damns a liar less than he who throws his life away for pride." Proctor also argues that, by refusing to save himself, he is neglecting his responsibility to his children.

Proctor desperately wants Elizabeth to agree to these arguments; by appealing to her, he tries to escape full responsibility for his actions. Proctor respects Elizabeth's strong sense of right and wrong. If she agrees, then he will feel morally justified in his confession.

Elizabeth, however, refuses to judge her husband. Instead, she simply states her love and confirms her faith in his goodness. She tells Proctor that he must make peace with himself; it is his soul, not her's, that he is risking.

Earlier, in Act II, Proctor had told his wife to "look to your own improvement before you go to judge your husband." Now Elizabeth heeds those words. While refusing to judge Proctor, she asks his forgiveness for her own sins of coldness and suspicion. Elizabeth's relentless honesty with herself tortures Proctor and forces him to realize his own lack of moral courage.

ACT IV • SCENE 5

Summary

Dawn has nearly arrived. Judge Hathorne returns and asks for Proctor's answer. Elizabeth pleads with Proctor to be true only to himself. Reluctantly, he agrees to confess. Hathorne, delighted, runs to bring the others. Elizabeth weeps, while Proctor clasps his hands and asks "God in Heaven, what is John Proctor, what is John Proctor?" He tries to believe that his confession is honest, because for him to die as a saint would be fraud. Finally he accepts that it is wrong: "Good, then — it is evil, and I do it!"

Danforth, Hale, Parris, Hathorne and Cheever enter. Cheever prepares to take down Proctor's confession, which will then be posted on the church door. Under Danforth's questioning, Proctor confesses to binding himself to the Devil's service.

Marshal Herrick brings Rebecca Nurse into the cell to witness the confession. Proctor turns his face to the wall, and refuses to testify that he has seen Rebecca, Martha Corey and others in the Devil's company. He tells Danforth that "I speak my own sins; I cannot judge another." Hale and Parris persuade Danforth to drop the matter, and to let Proctor sign his confession.

After Proctor reluctantly signs the paper, he snatches it out of Danforth's reach. Proctor begins to speak wildly as he realizes that his confession will be used against his friends on the very day that they are executed. He tells Danforth that it is enough that he has confessed. God does not need the confession made public to shame his sons, blacken the reputation of his friends and destroy his own good name.

Proctor cries out to Danforth that he will not hand over the confession "Because it is my name! . . . Because I lie and sign myself to lies! Because I am not worth the dust on the feet of them that hang!" Danforth tells him that there can be no compromise. If the confession is a lie, he wants no part of it. If it is honest, then Proctor must hand it over now. Weeping with fury, Proctor rips up the confession.

Against the frantic protests of Hale and Parris, Proctor triumphantly proclaims, "You have made your magic now, for now I do think I see some shred of goodness in John Proctor." He embraces Elizabeth passionately, and tells her not to cry, for "tears pleasure them." Danforth orders the hanging to begin, and sweeps out of the cell. Proctor and Rebecca are led away to the gallows by Herrick, while Hathorne and Cheever follow.

As Elizabeth watches the hanging through the barred window out of the cell, Parris and Hale beg her to run to Proctor and plead for him to change his mind. Elizabeth, nearing collapse, refuses to listen. As she grips the bars of the window, she cries, "He have his goodness now. God forbid I take it from him!" As the final drumroll announces that the hanging has taken place, Hale falls to his knees in frantic prayer. The morning sun pours in through the bars upon Elizabeth's face.

Commentary

Ever since his seduction of Abigail, Proctor has felt like a moral fraud. Many times in the play, he has refused to look honestly at his life, confront his weaknesses and accept responsibility for his actions.

In this scene, just before he confesses, Elizabeth tells him that he alone can judge his actions. He then cries "God in Heaven, what is John Proctor, what is John Proctor?" The final minutes of the play reveal an answer to that question, as John Proctor "finds his goodness."

Scene 5, then, can be seen as a moral journey in which Proctor learns that he must commit himself to the truth. At first, Proctor is in a state of complete moral confusion. One moment he claims that his confession is honest, for to die like a saint would be hypocritical. The next, he resigns himself to his moral weakness, and spits out that the confession "is evil, and I do it!"

Having agreed to confess, Proctor then tries to reach a series of compromises with himself. He confesses to several lies, but refuses to testify against anyone else. He cries out with hatred that "I cannot judge another . . . I have no tongue for it." Again, Danforth's insistence that Proctor name others who have conspired with the Devil is highly suggestive of the McCarthy hearings of the 1950s. In those hearings, many well-known and respected witnesses did not share Proctor's qualms. They informed willingly on their friends out of fear of the committee's power to damage their careers.

Proctor persuades Danforth to let him confess without testifying against others. He then tries to avoid signing his confession, arguing that a signature is not needed with so many witnesses. Under Danforth's orders, Proctor reluctantly signs, then snatches the paper away. Once again, he attempts to compromise, and refuses to hand over the signed confession. He tells Danforth that God does not need to see his name nailed to the church door.

In defending this compromise, Proctor reveals a great deal of moral confusion. He now knows that his signed confession will be used to strengthen the power of the court and blacken the memories of those who are about to die. Proctor is a proud man, and cannot bear to be used in this way. He also knows that the signed confession will destroy his good name and shame his children. Although he can live with the knowledge that he has betrayed his friends, he cannot stand the idea of public shame. He cries to Danforth that "I have given you my soul; leave me my name!"

As Danforth angrily tells Proctor, no compromise with the truth is possible. Proctor must either hand over his honest confession or hang. Rebecca Nurse, who has witnessed Proctor's confession, also refuses to compromise with the truth. When asked to confess, she answers that "it is a lie, it is a lie; how may I damn myself? I cannot." Rebecca and Danforth present the two extremes of good and evil, courage and cowardice, that Proctor must choose between. Once his commitment is made, there can be no turning back.

At last Proctor makes his choice and triumphantly tears up his confession. He commits himself totally to the truth, to loyalty for his friends and to the destruction of the court's authority. By refusing to abandon these values, Proctor regains the honor and integrity that he first lost with the seduction of Abigail. He has found himself, and can now declare that "I do think I see some shred of goodness in John Proctor. Not enough to weave a banner with, but white enough to keep it from such dogs."

As Proctor and Rebecca are led to the gallows, Hale and Parris beg Elizabeth to persuade her husband to change his mind. Parris pleads out of fear. He believes that the people of Salem will kill him in revenge for Proctor's and Rebecca's innocent deaths. Hale's motives are more complex. He believes that, if Proctor and Rebecca die, he will have killed them. Hale again argues that Proctor is throwing his life away out of pride, and begs Elizabeth to "Go to him, take his shame away." Elizabeth knows better: Proctor's death is not his shame but his honor. Out of love for her husband, she lets him die with his newly-found goodness intact.

ECHOES DOWN THE CORRIDOR

At the end of Act IV, Miller summarizes what later happened to some of the play's historical characters. Parris was voted out of office and driven from town. Abigail probably became a prostitute in Boston. Elizabeth Proctor remarried four years after Proctor's death.

Twenty years after the last execution, compensation was

awarded to the families of victims. However, many of the beneficiaries were not victims at all, but informers. In Salem, the excommunications were reversed.

In a final note, Miller states that, after the witch hunt, the power of the Puritan Church in Massachusetts was broken. Clearly, then, the lives of men and women like John Proctor and Rebecca Nurse were not wasted. Their courage and honesty prepared the way for greater freedom in the lives of those who followed them.

Character Sketches

The characters in *The Crucible* are based on real people who lived in Salem in 1692. In some cases, several people are fused into one or two characters. In addition, minor changes have been made to some of the details. In general, however, each character behaves much as his original behaved. Moreover, the ultimate fate of each character is the same as that of his historical counterpart.

Miller researched the Salem witch hunt exhaustively, and used historical records to base his drama as closely as possible on real events. This attention to historical accuracy lends an added force to *The Crucible* and intensifies our attitudes to each of the play's characters.

John Proctor

In his introduction to Proctor, Miller calls him "a man in his prime . . . with a quiet confidence and an unexpressed, hidden force." At the play's beginning, Proctor is well-respected in Salem for his good sense, honesty and even temper. He is not easily led by others. He must respect those in power before he follows their authority. He is hard-working and sober, and provides well for his family.

Yet, as he himself states, John Proctor is no saint. According to Miller, Proctor is "a sinner, not only against the moral fashion of the time, but against his own vision of decent conduct." Some months earlier, Proctor had seduced the 17-year-old Abigail Williams. As the play begins, he still lusts after her, although the affair is long over. Proctor's lechery leads to other weaknesses, including pride, dishonesty and moral cowardice. To escape public exposure, he delays testifying against Abigail until it is too late. When he finally does become involved, he makes every effort to evade his responsibilities until the last moments of his life.

The moral journey of John Proctor gives *The Crucible* its shape. At the play's beginning, Proctor has already adopted a vague stand against the authority of the church. Out of dislike for Reverend Parris' pettiness and greed, he has largely stopped attending prayer meetings and has refused to have his third child baptized. At this stage, Proctor thinks that he can carry on his rebellion quietly, by himself. He has no desire to become involved in any active opposition to the church, and he does not feel that the public good is any of his concern.

When Abigail and the other girls first spread rumors of witchcraft, Proctor knows they are lying to cover up their frolic in the woods. Rather than speak the truth, however, he simply retreats home in disgust, leaving Abigail to make her dangerous accusations without opposition.

For eight days, Proctor remains on his farm and refuses to pay any attention to the wild rumors, accusations and arrests that take place in Salem. Finally, Elizabeth forces him to take notice of events: a court has been formed and people are being sentenced to hang as witches. She tries to make him promise to denounce Abigail's testimony as lies. He refuses, out of fear that Abigail will expose him as a lecher.

When Mary Warren announces that Elizabeth has been "somewhat mentioned" in court, Proctor realizes reluctantly that he will have to denounce Abigail. The decision is not his own; he is forced into it by circumstances. When Elizabeth is arrested soon after, Proctor at last becomes determined to save her at any cost. However, despite his determination, he first attempts a variety of legal arguments to free his wife. He also bullies Mary into admitting to the court that the girls have been pretending.

When Abigail outwits him, Proctor finally has no choice but to denounce her as a harlot and confess that he is a lecher. He at last understands that, by holding back the truth and "quailing to bring men out of ignorance," he has committed a great wrong. His good name in shreds around him, Proctor is again outwitted by Abigail and is carried off to prison as a witch.

Proctor's moral journey is not yet complete. On the night before he is to be hanged, the court is desperate for his confession. Rebellion is spreading. To hold on to its power, the court needs one of its condemned prisoners to confess and thus blacken the good names of the others. So far, Proctor has resisted torture and refused out of pride to confess. Now he has talked himself into confessing with a number of arguments. He tells Elizabeth that it would be dishonest for him, a lecher and a sinner, to die like a saint.

Elizabeth tells Proctor that he must somehow make peace with himself. He asks the question that has tormented him

60

throughout: "What is John Proctor?" Proctor then tries to arrange a series of compromises with the truth. He will testify against himself, but not others. He will confess but not sign the confession. He will sign, but he won't hand it over.

Finally, Proctor realizes that no compromise is possible. If he wants to live, he must confess to lies and strengthen the court's authority by destroying the good names of his friends. In this moment of truth, Proctor tears up his confession and chooses to die honestly and with honor. As he walks to the gallows, his wife cries out, "He have his goodness now."

Like all of us, then, Proctor has many weaknesses. Yet, also like all of us, he has the potential for greatness. As Proctor confronts his weaknesses one by one he finds new strengths within himself. As the witch hunt progresses, he learns that no one can separate himself from the events of his time. He also comes to understand that truth cannot be compromised. Real honor can only be achieved through complete honesty and integrity.

Through his struggles to overcome the flaws in his character, Proctor at last finds the core of goodness within himself. As he walks to the gallows, he goes to a hero's death, not in spite of his weaknesses but because of them.

Elizabeth Proctor

Elizabeth is first described as sickly and cold. When we meet her, her relationship with her husband is clearly distant and strained. Elizabeth has taken it upon herself to act as Proctor's conscience. She has never really forgiven him for his adultery, and she accuses him of postponing his testimony against Abigail because he is still fond of the girl. Proctor replies to her criticisms by telling her to "look to your own improvement before you go to judge your husband any more."

Elizabeth's most admirable quality is her relentless honesty. She refuses to allow Proctor to shirk his responsibility to denounce the girls as liars. She tells Hale openly that she does not believe in witches, even though she knows that this will damage her case. After she is found guilty by the court, she refuses to make a false confession. And, when Proctor decides to confess, she helps him find the strength to change his mind and die with honor.

Ironically, Elizabeth's one lie proves to be her downfall. In order to protect Proctor from the court, she denies that he is a lecher. Unfortunately, Proctor's case against Abigail is based upon his confession of lechery. Elizabeth's lie, far from protecting her husband, leads to his arrest and conviction.

Through the course of the play, Elizabeth's character undergoes certain changes. At first she seems weak, cold and unforgiving. Then, when she is first arrested, she reveals a strength and dignity that are admirable. During her months in prison, she has plenty of time to search her soul. When she sees Proctor at the end of the play, she asks his forgiveness. She has indeed looked to her own improvement, and now recognizes that "it were a cold house I kept!" Elizabeth's honesty with herself inspires Proctor, and helps him to find his own integrity.

Elizabeth Proctor, then, functions as a model of honesty, dignity, courage and integrity. She is a direct contrast to Abigail Williams. The fact that Elizabeth is put in prison while Abigail is treated like a saint shows the extent to which Salem's social order has been turned upside down by the witch hunt. At the end of *The Crucible*, Elizabeth makes a sacrifice that Abigail could never have made. For love of Proctor, and for the common good, she lets her husband die.

Abigail Williams

It is tempting to view Abigail as evil incarnate. When we meet her, she has already tempted Proctor into lechery and begun to plot against Elizabeth's life. She is a vain, scheming, vengeful bully, who easily forces her will on the other girls. To escape punishment for dancing, she does not care how many lives she ruins. Later, as she grows in power and influence, she seems to enjoy sending many innocent people to their deaths. Abigail has no moral sense. She takes pleasure in her lies, and thrives on the attention and power that they bring her.

Nonetheless, it is impossible to totally condemn Abigail. Life in the extremely rigid and repressed society of the Puritans is clearly unbearable for a bright, high-spirited girl of 17. Abigail loves pleasure, and pleasure is strictly forbidden in Salem. Indeed, games, entertainments, holidays and fun of just about any kind are not only sinful but against the law. It is easy to see why Abigail has come to despise the solemn Puritans as hypocrites and why she enjoys their transformation into hysterical witch hunters. It is also easy to see why she thrives on the attention she receives as the center of the excitement; among the high-minded Puritans, young girls were neither to be seen nor heard.

Whatever one thinks of Abigail, it is impossible to deny her great creativity as a liar. The performance with which she forces Mary Warren to take back her testimony is a *tour de force*. Abigail's imagination, intelligence and powers as an actress are very great indeed. In another society, these talents might have been encouraged. In Salem, however, they were rigidly repressed, and they finally exploded.

Reverend John Hale

For Reverend Hale, as for John Proctor, the witch hunt in Salem is the scene of a moral journey. Hale first arrives in Salem as a confident, naive expert on witches, looking forward to trying out his new skills in a face-to-face battle with Satan. Because of his eagerness, however, Hale puts words into the mouths of the girls, and unknowingly encourages them to lie. In a sense, Hale is responsible for getting the witch hunt underway and setting the stage for the girls' wild lies and accusations.

In Act II, when respected citizens have started to be accused in the court, Hale begins to doubt the girl's testimony. Although he has so far resisted the suspicion, he has also begun to think that many people have confessed simply to keep from hanging. Hale finally decides to meet some of the accused himself, "without the court's authority."

Hale visits the Proctors and is impressed with their honesty. Nonetheless, he refuses to believe Proctor's statement that Abigail is lying. When Elizabeth is arrested, Hale does nothing to intervene and claims that the court will be just. Proctor calls Hale a "Pontius Pilate" and a coward, and drives him from the house.

In Act III, Hale can no longer hide his doubts about the court's justice. Just that morning, he had signed the death warrant of the virtuous Rebecca Nurse, and his "hand shakes yet as with a wound." When Proctor denounces Abigail, Hale believes him, and urges the court to listen. As Abigail and the girls stage a performance to discredit Proctor, Hale sees through the act and protests. Proctor is arrested, and Hale realizes that he is partly to blame. He denounces the court and leaves, slamming the door behind him.

In the final act, Hale is a broken man. He has listened to his conscience too late to save the lives of those he has condemned to die. As he tells Elizabeth, "what I touched with my bright confidence, it died; and where I turned the eye of my great faith, blood flowed up." Now Hale will do anything to stem the flow of that blood, including damning his own soul by advising the condemned to make false confessions and save themselves.

Hale cannot escape his guilt so easily, however. By advising prisoners to confess, he is strengthening the power of the court by postponing rebellion. The prisoners know this, and will not do as he asks. Although John Proctor weakens, he too ultimately decides to die with honor. As the prisoners go to the gallows, Hale is left weeping on his knees, a tragic example of an honest man who blindly believed in authority until it was too late.

Deputy Governor Danforth

In many ways, Deputy Governor Danforth is the model Puritan, unbending, humorless and devout. He holds fervently to the strict letter of the law and takes every word of the Bible literally. As the Chief Justice of Massachusetts, Danforth is in charge of the administration of "God's law." He believes that he acts in God's place and can do no wrong. Therefore he believes that anyone who questions his authority, also questions the authority of God and the church.

Unfortunately, these characteristics combine to produce a moral monster. Because Danforth takes the Bible literally, he blindly believes that witches exist and must be destroyed. Because he believes that he acts with God's authority, he willingly suspends due process of law and relies on hysterical girls and false confessions for the truth. Once embarked on this course, he cannot turn back. To admit that he has been mistaken would be to admit that God could err. As a result, many innocent people are sent to their deaths.

Although Danforth is a pompous, self-deceiving fool, he is neither a hypocrite nor a coward. Unlike Parris, he refuses to favor the powerful and wealthy over the poor and the outcast. Also unlike Parris, he does not fear retribution for his actions. He declares bravely that he "should hang ten thousand that dared rise against the law." In addition, Danforth is honest. He will not accept a confession of lies from Proctor, no matter how useful it would be to him.

Reverend Samuel Parris

As Miller states, "there is very little good to be said" for Reverend Parris. Indeed, it is difficult to describe him with anything but a list of faults. As the minister, Parris is the major religious and legal administrator in Salem. His corrupt behavior suggests that the Puritan theocracy is already crumbling. Indeed, it is Parris who first drives Proctor away from the church's authority.

Parris is totally self-serving. When we first meet him, he is less frightened by his daughter's illness than by how it will reflect on him. His life is a series of petty, selfish concerns; he wants his firewood for free and the deed to the minister's house. His mind is more often on material than spiritual matters. As Proctor tells Hale, "for twenty week he preach nothin' but golden candlesticks until he had them."

Parris is also a deeply suspicious man, and believes that Proctor and others are plotting against him. With the witch hunt, Parris sees his chance to strengthen his power over the town. He becomes fanatical in his relentless persecution of "witches," and continually fuels the hysteria that grips Salem.

Eventually, Parris' zeal defeats him. As the people begin to rebel against the court, his own life is threatened. Abigail steals his savings and runs away, leaving him penniless. In terror for his life, Parris now tries to undo what he has done. He begs Proctor and Rebecca to confess and save themselves. As the prisoners walk to the gallows, Parris runs after them, pleading for his life, barely worthy of contempt.

Plot

The plot of *The Crucible* exists on two levels: outer and inner. On the broad, outer level, the play offers a complex portrait of the tragedy of an entire society. Through the actions of 21 characters, the Salem witch hunt is presented from its start to its near-finish.

In Act I, the source of "the delusion" is traced to the spite and hysteria of a few young girls. These initial flames are then fueled by vengeance, greed and the thirst for power of the Puritan theocracy. In Act II, the hysteria is spread to the point where respected citizens are arrested. In Act III, the trials are exposed as travesties of justice, in which innocent people are condemned on the basis of the transparent lies of children and the false confessions of frightened witnesses. Finally, Act IV explores the dilemma faced by those who must choose between a false confession and death with honor.

Against this broad sweep of events, the inner plot of *The Crucible* also unfolds. At the beginning of the play, John Proctor has already fallen from grace through the crime of lechery. The stumbling search for his lost integrity takes Proctor through a personal rejection of his church, disharmony in his home, the arrest of his wife, a confrontation with corrupt authority, a courtroom battle, and imprisonment and torture as a witch. Finally, it leads him to choose death with honor over life with dishonor.

The inner voyage of John Proctor is echoed and contrasted by that of Reverend Hale. In Act I, Hale has absolute faith in the authority of the church and is confident in his role as inquisitor. By Act II, doubts have set in, though Hale resists them. The absurdities of the trial in Act III force Hale to finally lose faith in the court. Like Proctor, Hale listens to his conscience too late. He quits the court, but only after signing 72 death warrants. In Act IV, Hale is a broken man. To ease his terrible burden of guilt, he advises prisoners to live at any cost, even that of their own souls.

The plot of *The Crucible*, then, interweaves a broad depiction of historical events with a close look at the moral development of John Proctor and, to a lesser extent, Reverend Hale. John Proctor is easy for the audience to identify with as he searches for "his goodness." Through this identification, the audience is drawn into the play and becomes directly immersed in the social tragedy that took place in Salem in 1692.

Themes

The Crucible presents two major themes. The first concerns the responsibility of each individual to take a stand against the abuses of authority in his society. The second involves the individual's search for integrity, for a sense of himself that he can live with. Of course, these themes are interwoven throughout the play, and are only separated here for the purposes of study.

Personal Responsibility versus Authority

As Arthur Miller is careful to explain, the Puritan government's total religious and political authority was necessary at first to help the colony survive against great odds. Hard work, rigid discipline and a devotion to the Puritan ethic all had to be strictly enforced in the face of a bitter climate and a dangerous wilderness. Anyone who challenged the power of the church at that time was indeed posing a serious threat to the welfare of the community.

By 1692, however, the wilderness was no longer so dangerous and frightening. Some Puritans began to feel that the church's absolute power was no longer justified. Dissent began to breed confusion and threaten the social order, and the church began to look for new ways to hold onto its authority. In this uncertain social climate, the first cries of witchcraft were heard. Soon the prisons of Massachusetts were full of "witches," innocent victims of a theocracy gone out of control.

Act I of *The Crucible* quickly establishes that the church's authority in Salem is corrupt. Reverend Parris is a weak, self-serving minister, who worries as much about the cost of his firewood as the health of his daughter. He ingratiates himself with the wealthy Putnams while imagining that Proctor and others are conspiring against him. In a fit of petulance, he tells Proctor that "There is either obedience or the church will burn like Hell is burning!"

Proctor cannot accept this need for obedience. As he tells Rebecca, "I like not the smell of this authority." Yet so far Proctor's protest is limited to a personal dislike of Parris. It is an asocial protest, and takes the form of absence from prayer services and town meetings. Proctor makes no attempt to seriously challenge Parris' authority. By simply quarrelling with

Parris and retreating in anger to his farm, he behaves irresponsibly, as Rebecca Nurse warns.

In Act II, Proctor is reluctantly drawn out of his isolation to confront the alarming events that are taking place in Salem. Abigail has told Proctor that the talk of witchcraft has no basis in truth. For eight days, he has looked the other way while several arrests have been made. Now Elizabeth urges him to denounce Abigail before she becomes too powerful. Proctor hesitates, because he knows that in the process he might have to confess to lechery. Even after his servant returns and he learns the extent of the madness in Salem, he is unwilling to become involved.

The actions of Reverend Hale serve to bring Proctor's behavior into clearer focus. Reverend Hale had arrived in Salem brimming with confidence in the church's power and righteousness. He had then proceeded to put words into the girls' mouths and to inspire the first accusations of witchcraft. Now that respected farmers are being arrested, he has begun to doubt the truth of these accusations. Acting on his own authority, he has come to meet the Proctors for himself. However, at this stage, Hale continues to speak for the church and criticizes Proctor for quarreling with Parris; "The man's ordained, therefore the light of God is in him."

When Herrick and Cheever arrive to arrest Elizabeth, neither Proctor nor Hale can any longer ignore the perversion of the court's authority. To different degrees, Herrick and Cheever each plead that they are only following orders; this is the cry of the Nazi war criminal, a cry that echoes wherever weak men knowingly serve evil authority. Hale reassures Proctor that "the court is just," but he has begun to disbelieve it himself. Proctor turns on Hale, calling him a "Pontius Pilate" who seeks to wash his hands of responsibility to the truth. Yet, for eight days, Proctor himself has avoided that same responsibility.

In Act III, Proctor attempts to free Elizabeth and disprove Abigail's testimony in court. He still hopes to avoid any personal dishonor, and presents various briefs along with the testimony of Mary Warren. Only when he is totally out-maneuvered by Abigail does he finally commit himself and confess to lechery. Again he is out-maneuvered, and he is arrested as a witch. Hale, who has watched the proceedings with increasing frustration, finally must listen to his conscience, and he quits the court.

Deputy Governor Danforth and Judge Hathorne represent the authority of the Puritan church throughout Massachusetts. As Chief Justice, Danforth is the embodiment of "God's law" with all its bigotry, rigidity and intolerance of opposition. Due process has been abandoned in the court's attempt "to discover what no one has ever seen." The rules of evidence have been discarded for superstition, hearsay, hysteria and fear. Under Danforth, opportunists like Abigail and Putnam have twisted the law into a weapon for vengeance and land greed. So far, 72 innocent people have been condemned to die.

At one point in the trial, Danforth states that "a person is either with this court or he must be counted against it, there be no road between." As both Proctor and Hale come to understand, this statement is true. Each of them might have been able to prevent the witch hunt if he had acted earlier to oppose the court's authority. As Proctor is dragged from the court he recognizes that, by failing to involve himself until it was too late, he must accept some of the responsibility for the taking of innocent lives: "For them that quail to bring men out of ignorance, as I have quailed, and as you quail now . . . God damns our kind especially, and we will burn, we will burn together!"

By Act IV, the court's abuse of its power has plunged Salem into chaos. Orphans roam the streets hungry, farmers fight over abandoned cattle, and people everywhere live in terror for their lives. Rebellion has broken out close by, and shows signs of spreading. Several respected citizens are scheduled to hang at dawn, and unless one of them confesses, the hanging may prove to be the spark that ignites rebellion in Salem.

In order to break the court's corrupt authority, then, the condemned prisoners will have to sacrifice their lives. Rebecca Nurse understands this, and is already "one foot in Heaven." For Proctor, the decision is more difficult. He attempts a series of compromises in which he confesses but tries to prevent the court from using his confession to strengthen its power. But these tactics fail and Proctor realizes that he too must die in order to weaken the court's authority.

As Proctor weighs his decision, Reverend Hale urges him to confess and live. With so much blood on his own head, Hale has decided that "no principle, however glorious" can justify further bloodshed. In his effort to ease his guilt, Hale now serves the very authority he despises by discouraging the heroic acts that would bring the court tumbling to its knees. Hale is a broken man. Having damned his own soul, he now counsels others to damn theirs.

Proctor ignores Hale, and chooses to die as the ultimate gesture against the tyranny of the court. As Proctor mounts the gallows, Hale begs Elizabeth to stop him: "What profit him to bleed? Shall the dust praise him? Shall the worms declare his truth?" It is a measure of Hale's moral blindness that he assumes the answers to these questions to be no. As Miller tells us, the deaths of Proctor, Rebecca and others were instrumental in breaking the power of the Puritan theocracy.

Miller's message, then, is clear. Every individual is responsible for the welfare of society. Those who do not actively oppose tyranny, support it. As Danforth claims, "there be no road between." Freedom is a gift more precious than life. Those who enjoy it must be on guard constantly to protect it from the abuses of power.

First staged in 1953, *The Crucible* was intended by Miller as a comment on the McCarthy hearings that were then taking place. Under McCarthyism, as in Salem, due process of law had been abandoned. Innocent people were tormented on the basis of hearsay and rumor. Justice was turned upside down in a search for the Red Devil that had stolen the souls of Americans. Careers were shattered and lives were ruined. Few people had the courage to challenge Washington's authority.

The McCarthy hearings are well behind us, yet *The Crucible* continues to be one of Miller's most popular plays. Clearly, no age is free of the struggle between freedom and authority. Strong, courageous men and women are always needed to challenge the abuse of power. Ultimately, the need for social responsibility is a timeless theme.

The Search for Integrity

The first theme of *The Crucible* places the individual into conflict with his society. The second theme, on the other hand, places him in conflict with himself. According to Miller, *The Crucible* is a close look at "the conflict between a man's raw deeds and his conception of himself." John Proctor is tormented by this conflict. Throughout the play, he struggles against his own weaknesses to achieve a view of himself that he can accept. This battle for integrity is lost many times before it is finally won in the play's last minutes.

When Proctor clasps his hands in the last act and pleads, "God in Heaven, what is John Proctor, what is John Proctor," he is voicing a question that has driven him from the beginning. When we first meet Proctor, he has already lost respect for himself as a result of his adultery with Abigail. His crime has been compounded by dishonesty; in presenting himself as an upright citizen of Salem, he considers himself a fraud. He does not feel that he deserves his good name.

In Salem, a person's name, or reputation, is everything. It binds contracts, seals loyalties and sums up the moral strength of its owner to the community. A person's name is a measure of how well he is thought of by his neighbors. It also stands for its owner's ideals and values. In Proctor's case, those ideals are honesty and loyalty. He has already lied, and soon he will contemplate betraying his friends.

Although Proctor does not feel entitled to his good name, he has no desire to lose it. When Abigail first starts calling people witches, Proctor knows she is lying. To denounce her, however, he would risk being exposed as a lecher, and his good name in Salem would be ruined. By refusing to risk his reputation, Proctor allows Abigail's power to grow unchecked. Finally, his own wife is arrested for witchcraft.

To defend Elizabeth, Proctor swears to "fall like an ocean on that court." Nonetheless, he continues to postpone putting his name on the line. Eventually, when all other methods fail, he sees no other way to denounce Abigail. Trembling, "his life collapsing about him," he confesses to lechery. The price is high: "I have made a bell of my honor! I have rung the doom of my good name —."

Ironically, Elizabeth's concern for Proctor's name causes her to temporarily abandon her own integrity and deny that he is a lecher. This denial sets in motion the events that lead to Proctor's arrest. Too late, Proctor realizes the damage he has done by failing to confront Abigail earlier: "For them that quail to bring men out of ignorance, as I have quailed . . . God damns our kind especially."

At this stage, Proctor has lost sight of his honor entirely. Out of fear for his reputation, he has allowed tyranny to spread through Salem. This crime, combined with lechery, dishonesty and false pride, damns Proctor in his own eyes. As far as he is concerned, his soul is lost.

When we next meet Proctor, he has been imprisoned for three months. Although he has withstood torture out of pride, he now plans to make a false confession. He tells Elizabeth that he would be a fraud to die like Rebecca and others who have refused to confess: "My honesty is broke, Elizabeth; I am no good man. Nothing's spoiled by giving them this lie that were not rotten long before."

Elizabeth refuses to judge Proctor. She urges him to find the goodness within himself: "It is not my soul, John, it is yours." She calls him a good man, and blames herself for his weakness: "It needs a cold wife to prompt lechery." Proctor refuses to accept this assessment, but the example of Elizabeth's integrity is not lost on him. Ripping away all pretense and rationalization, he forces himself to confront the truth: "Good then — it is evil, and I do it."

Although Proctor thinks that he has given himself over to evil, there are lengths to which he will not go. His loyalty proves greater than he believes it to be. He refuses to testify against others: "I like not to spoil their names." He also refuses to hand over his signed confession for the court's use against his friends: "I blacken all of them when this is nailed to the church the very day they hang for silence."

Although Proctor knows he is damned in the eyes of God, he cannot bear to be damned in the eyes of his neighbors. In the climactic speech of the play, he cries that he cannot hand over the confession "Because it is my name! Because I cannot have another in my life! . . . I have given you my soul; leave me my name!" Throughout the play, Proctor has separated his soul from his name and his actions from his ideals. His soul was first lost the moment he seduced Abigail, and his efforts to protect his name only drove his soul further from him.

In order to achieve integrity, Proctor's soul and his name must become one. No compromise is possible, as Danforth tells him, "You will give me your honest confession in my hand, or I cannot keep you from the rope." Finally, weeping in fury, Proctor seizes hold of his honor as he tears up the false confession.

As Proctor prepares to die for loyalty and truth, he at last finds a worthy answer to the question "What is John Proctor?" Although he knows he is no saint, he can now at least "see some shred of goodness" in himself. By choosing death over dishonor, Proctor has regained his soul. As he walks to the gallows, Elizabeth refuses to interfere with her husband's new-found integrity: "He have his goodness now. God forbid I take it from him."

Structure

Because *The Crucible* is based on an actual period of history, it poses special structural challenges for the playwright. It is difficult to write a tight, coherent play that uses more than 20 characters and spans several months of time. In *The Crucible*, Miller meets these challenges, and creates a highly organized structure within which to present the broad sweep of historical events.

To overcome the problems posed by the historical scope of the Salem witch hunt, Miller has concentrated the essence of the period into four moments in time at four different places. This has allowed him to maintain the classical unities of Time, Place and Action within each of *The Crucible*'s four acts. Each act has its own coherent structure. Its events occur in one setting only and take place in real time. There are no jumps from place to place or time lapses to break up the action. Time shifts only occur between the acts, and are also accompanied by changes in setting.

To further enhance unity in the play, Miller has made each act follow a similar pattern of development. In each case, the act begins quite calmly as characters discuss events in relative peace. As the act moves forward, feelings become increasingly intense until they finally erupt in a series of emotional outbursts. By its end, the act always attains a frenzied emotional pitch: Act I ends with the girls' first fevered accusations; Act II with Proctor's rage at Elizabeth's arrest; Act III with Proctor's own highly-emotional arrest; and Act IV with the executions of the condemned.

To show how the population of an entire town reacts to the witch hunt, Miller introduces a great many characters into the play. However, even 21 people are not really enough to provide the historical scope Miller is aiming for. In order to increase the number of individuals available to him without making the play more difficult to stage, Miller relies on a number of offstage characters through the conversations of others. Martha Corey and Ruth Putnam are two examples of offstage characters. Another example takes place at the beginning of Act III when we overhear Giles Corey disrupting the trial; the illusion is crreated of an entire offstage courtroom brimming with townspeople, eager participants in the witch hunt.

Although *The Crucible* has many characters, it only concentrates on one of them in great depth. John Proctor is the play's major unifying element. In his search for integrity amid the madness of Salem, he focuses *The Crucible*'s plot and develops its two major themes. Proctor invites the audience to identify with him and to view the witch hunt through his eyes. In conflict with himself and with society, Proctor's moral journey to self-realization provides the overall structural framework of the play.

In essence, this framework follows the time-honored pattern of the well-made play. The first scenes provide the background to the witch hunt and introduce us to the play's key characters. The rising action gets underway as the girls raise the first dangerous accusations. For Proctor, the rising action takes the form of greater and greater disruption of his life. This continues through the trouble in his marriage, intensifies with the arrest of his wife and culminates in the absurdity and horror of the courtroom trial.

The play reaches a turning point when Elizabeth's testimony inadvertently leads to Proctor's arrest. In the last act, the play's falling action moves events toward their inevitable climax. When Proctor tears up his confession, his self-discovery is finally complete. A brief denouement follows this climax, as Elizabeth watches her husband mount the gallows.

Some critics have criticized *The Crucible* for being one act too long, suggesting that the play should have ended with the arrest of Proctor in Act III. However, these critics fail to recognize that the play's structure is based on Proctor's search for honor and self-respect. At the end of Act III, Proctor has not yet found "his goodness." His struggle with himself continues right to the moment when he tears up his confession and chooses death over dishonor.

Setting

The Crucible is set in Puritan New England in 1692. As we have already seen, Miller researched this period in great depth in an attempt to make his portrait of Salem life as authentic as possible. Not only are the characters closely based on real people, but their conversations often echo statements found in historical records and court transcripts.

As early settlers in New England, the Puritans lived the frugal lives of pioneers. Houses were built of logs, wood fires provided the only heat for cooking or warmth, and kerosene lamps or candles offered the only light after dark. When John Proctor enters his home with a rifle in Act II, it is a reminder that the dangerous wilderness begins just beyond the boundaries of the Proctor farm.

The Puritans were somber, disciplined people who did not allow any frivolity to come between them and their work. Each of the settings in The Crucible reflects the spartan quality of Salem life. Furnishings of any kind are kept to a minimum and always serve a definite purpose. Decoration for its own sake simply does not exist. In general, the rooms are described as spare, tidy and plain. The descriptions give the sense of hard beds and stiff, uncomfortable benches and chairs.

In order to achieve the greatest possible unity in his play, Miller gave each of his four acts unity of Place, with each occurring entirely within one setting only. Because each of these settings is different, the play can offer four different views of life in Salem. To some degree, the settings in The Crucible comment on one another. The orderly calm of the Proctors' home, for example, is in clear contrast to the emotional chaos in Parris' home. And the dark, filthy prison cell is a strong rebuke to the hypocrisy of the austere courtroom antechamber.

Act I takes place in the bedroom of Betty Parris. The room is small, as is the window, which lets in only a little of the morning sun. The room is sparsely furnished: a bed, a chair, a chest, a small table and a candle. Because the house is not very old, the "wood colors are raw and unmellowed."

Clearly, this is not a pleasant room for a child. There is nothing to play with, nothing to look at and nothing to stimulate the imagination. Yet, as The Crucible clearly shows, the imagination of young girls can never be totally repressed.

76

Indeed, in this bare, dark, uncomfortable room, the girls invent their first extravagant lies.

Act II is set in the "common room" of the Proctors' house. The common room is a combination kitchen, living room and dining room. Here almost all household activities except sleeping take place. The room is clean and tidy, though rather dark and somber. When we first see it, Elizabeth is upstairs singing gently to her children. Dinner is cooking over an open fire.

The quiet of the Proctors' home is a welcome relief from the hysterical atmosphere of Betty Parris' bedroom. Yet, even here there are signs that life is not as pleasant as it could be. As Proctor enters the room, he tastes the stew in the fireplace and finds it bland. Later, he suggests to Elizabeth that she "bring some flowers in the house," as it is spring. Elizabeth's failure to make her home more warm and attractive is partly behind the guilt she feels in Act IV, when she confesses to her husband that "It were a cold house I kept!"

Despite its shortcomings, the Proctors' home at the beginning of Act II is harmonious and orderly. Throughout the act, this domestic tranquility becomes increasingly disrupted. First, Proctor and Elizabeth quarrel. Then Mary arrives with disturbing news. Then Hale arrives to question Elizabeth. Finally, Elizabeth is arrested, and Proctor is left behind, half-mad with grief and rage. Despite Proctor's attempt to retreat from society, the hysteria that has gripped Salem has finally plunged his own private world into chaos.

Act III takes place in the vestry of the Salem meetinghouse, which is now the anteroom of the Salem General Court. The room is described as "solemn, even forbidding" with heavy exposed roofbeams. There are two plain benches, a long meeting table with stools and one armchair. Sunlight pours through two high windows. Offstage in the courtroom, a trial is taking place.

As the act begins, we overhear the trial of Martha Corey. As Martha denies the charges against her and Giles is thrown out for creating a disturbance, we gain a vivid impression of a packed courtroom during a highly sensational public trial. As the voices of the townspeople rise excitedly, the door opens and Giles Corey is carried into the room by Herrick.

The meetinghouse, or church, of Salem has been turned

into a court. This underlines the fact that, in the Puritan theocracy, the church and the state were the same. Just as the Puritans believed that God presided over their church services, they believed that He watched over their legal matters. A solemn, forbidding atmosphere was therefore considered appropriate for both.

In the severe atmosphere created by this setting, we meet the equally severe Puritan authorities, Deputy Governor Danforth and Judge Hathorne. We quickly learn however that, for all its apparent loftiness and austerity, Puritan justice is an absurd and horrific farce. Eventually, the solemn atmosphere of the setting is turned completely upside down by the bizarre performances of Abigail and the girls. When Hale leaves the room in disgust, he slams the door behind him, thereby turning his back on Puritan authority and all it stands for.

Unlike the vestry room of the court, the setting for Act IV has no pretensions at all. The final act of *The Crucible* is set in a bleak prison cell shortly before sunrise. Moonlight trickles through a barred window. There are two benches and a great, heavy door. Early in the act, Danforth comments on the cell's "prodigious stench."

The setting for Act IV, then, is one of total squalor and desolation. In vile cells like this one, many of the finest people in Salem wait to be executed. Yet, in this foul setting, John Proctor finds the honor and integrity to choose death over a false confession. In Act III, a dignified setting was made lowly and absurd by the evil accusations of the court; in Act IV, a sordid setting is ennobled by the courage and honesty of the prisoners.

Throughout Act IV, the cell is dark except for Herrick's lantern and the faint moonlight. However, just as Act I of *The Crucible* began in the morning, Act IV ends with the first light of dawn. Events have come full circle: the witch hunt has been launched, reached its peak, and now, due to the courage of Proctor, Rebecca, and others, it is about to come to a close. As Elizabeth watches her husband's execution through the barred window of the cell, "the new sun" pours in upon her face, symbolizing a new era of freedom from tyranny in Salem.

Dramatic Language

In order to create the atmosphere of 17th century Salem, Miller has invented a special dialect for his characters. In some cases, speeches in *The Crucible* are based directly on historical records and court documents. For example, in Appendix One, a court record shows the following exchange in the trial of Sarah Good:

Q. Why do you hurt these children?
A. I do not hurt them. I scorn it.

And in *The Crucible*, at the beginning of Act III, Judge Hathorne is overheard questioning Martha Corey:

Hathorne's Voice: Why do you hurt these children?
Martha Corey's Voice: I do not hurt them. I scorn it!

Although the language in *The Crucible* sounds authentic, it is not really early colonial English. Language has changed a great deal in three hundred years, and an audience today would find it difficult to follow a real 17th century conversation. As Miller himself has stated:

I use words like "poppet" instead of "doll," and grammatical syntax like "he have" instead of "he has." This will remind the audience that *The Crucible* is taking place in another time, but won't make it too difficult to understand, which it might be if I used all the old language, with words like "dafter" instead of "daughter."

Because the dialect in *The Crucible* is unfamiliar to us and not meant to be realistic, it is free to become highly lyrical. For example, when John Proctor describes the spring landscape, he says "Lilacs have a purple smell. Lilac is the smell of nightfall, I think. Massachusetts is a beauty in the spring." And when he rages at the sky after Elizabeth's arrest, he cries, "We are only what we always were, but naked now . . . Aye, naked! And the wind, God's icy wind, will blow!"

Language in *The Crucible* becomes most stylized and exotic

in the false "trances" of Abigail and the other girls. Abigail's first accusations are rich with poetry. The strong rhythm created in the following speech is based on the repetition of sentences beginning with "I":

> Abigail: I want to open myself! . . . I want the light of God, I want the sweet love of Jesus! I danced for the Devil; I saw him; I wrote in his book; I go back to Jesus; I kiss His hand. I saw Sarah Good with the Devil! I saw Goody Osburn with the Devil! I saw Bridget Bishop with the Devil!

In a later scene, Abigail again uses repetition to achieve her purposes. By echoing every word that Mary Warren says, she convinces the court that Mary's spirit has possessed her. The effect is eerie, and very powerful dramatically.

In *The Crucible*, complex, emotional speeches often conceal deceit or false reasoning. The truth is simple, and needs no rhetoric to adorn it. The most striking example of this contrast occurs when Hale asks Elizabeth to persuade her husband to confess. In a series of beautifully phrased arguments, Hale maintains that there is nothing worth dying for: "Life, woman, life is God's most precious gift; no principle, however glorious, may justify the taking of it." Elizabeth listens to Hale's claims, then rejects them quietly and simply: "I think that be the Devil's argument."

Because the stylized language in *The Crucible* easily lends itself to moments of intense lyricism, it is ideal for portraying the inner struggle of John Proctor. Throughout the witch hunt, Proctor's spiritual anguish erupts in bursts of poetry. In the climactic speech of the play, Proctor teeters on the edge of abandoning his honor once and for all. He finds, however, that he cannot bring himself to hand over his signed confession:

> Proctor, *with a cry of his whole soul:* Because it is my name! Because I cannot have another in my life! Because I lie and sign myself to lies! Because I am not worth the dust on the feet of them that hang! How may I live without my name? I have given you my soul; leave me my name!

At the end of this speech, Proctor finally realizes that, to mean anything, his name must reflect his soul. He tears his confession into shreds and chooses a heroic death.

*Arthur Miller on *The Crucible*

One afternoon last week I attended a rehearsal of the imminent Off Broadway production of *The Crucible*. For the first time in the five years since its opening on Broadway, I heard its dialogue, and the experience awakened not merely memories but the desire to fire a discussion among us of certain questions a play like this ought to have raised.

Notoriously, there is what is called a chemistry in the theatre, a fusion of play, performance, and audience temper which, if it does not take place, leaves the elements of an explosion cold and to one side of art. For the critics, this seems to be what happened with *The Crucible*. It was not condemned; it was set aside. A cold thing, mainly, it lay to one side of entertainment, to say nothing of art. In a word, I was told that I had not written another *Death of a Salesman*.

It is perhaps beyond my powers to make clear, but I had no desire to write another *Salesman*, and not because I lack love for that play but for some wider, less easily defined reasons that have to do with this whole question of cold and heat, and, indeed, with the future of our drama altogether. It is the question of whether we—playwrights and audiences and critics—are to declare that we have reached the end, the last development of dramatic form. More specifically, the play designed to draw a tear; the play designed to "identify" the audience with its characters in the usual sense; the play that takes as its highest challenge the emotional relations of the family, for that, as it turns out, is what it comes to.

I was disappointed in the reaction to *The Crucible* not only for the obvious reasons but because no critic seemed to sense what I was after. In 1953 McCarthyism probably helped to make it appear that the play was bounded on all sides by its arraignment of the witch hunt. The political trajectory was so clear—a fact of which I am a little proud—that what to me were equally if not more important elements were totally ignored. The new production, appearing in a warmer climate, may, I hope, flower,

*Editor's title. From "Brewed in *The Crucible*." From *The New York Times*, March 9, 1958, II, p. 3. The Off Broadway revival which occasioned this article opened at the Martinique on March 11, 1958. Directed by Ward Baker, the production ran for more than a year and closed on June 14, 1959, after 633 performances. The production used a narrator, called The Reader, to set the scenes and give the historical background of the play.

and these inner petals may make their appropriate appearance.

What I say now may appear more technical than a writer has any business talking about in public. But I do not think it merely a question of technique to say that with all its excellences the kind of play we have come to accept without effort or question is standing at a dead end. What "moves" us is coming to be a narrower and narrower aesthetic fragment of life. I have shown, I think, that I am not unaware of psychology or immune to the fascinations of the neurotic hero, but I believe that it is no longer possible to contain the truth of the human situation so totally within a single man's guts as the bulk of our plays presuppose. The documentation of man's loneliness is not in itself and for itself ultimate wisdom, and the form this documentation inevitably assumes in playwriting is not the ultimate dramatic form.

I was drawn to write *The Crucible* not merely as a response to McCarthyism. It is not any more an attempt to cure witch hunts than *Salesman* is a plea for the improvement of conditions for travelling men, *All My Sons* a plea for better inspection of airplane parts, or *A View from the Bridge* an attack upon the Immigration Bureau. *The Crucible* is, internally, *Salesman*'s blood brother. It is examining the questions I was absorbed with before—the conflict between a man's raw deeds and his conception of himself; the question of whether conscience is in fact an organic part of the human being, and what happens when it is handed over not merely to the state or the mores of the time but to one's friend or wife. The big difference, I think, is that *The Crucible* sought to include a higher degree of consciousness than the earlier plays.

I believe that the wider the awareness, the felt knowledge, evoked by a play, the higher it must stand as art. I think our drama is far behind our lives in this respect. There is a lot wrong with the twentieth century, but one thing is right with it—we are aware as no generation was before of the larger units that help make us and destroy us. The city, the nation, the world, and now the universe are never far beyond our most intimate sense of life. The vast majority of us know now—not merely as knowledge but as feeling, feeling capable of expression in art—that we are being formed, that our alternatives in life are not absolutely our own, as the romantic play inevitably must presuppose. But the response of our plays, of our dramatic form itself, is to faint, so to speak, before the intricacies of man's wider relationships and to define him further and redefine him as essentially alone in a world he never made.

The form, the shape, the meaning of *The Crucible* were all compounded out of the faith of those who were hanged. They were asked to be lonely and they refused. They were asked to deny their belief in a God of all men, not merely a god each individual could manipulate to his interests. They were asked to call a phantom real and to deny their touch with reality. It was not good to cast this play, to form it so that the psyche of the hero should emerge so "commonly" as to wipe out of mind the process itself, the spectacle of that faith and the knowing will which these people paid for with their lives.

The "heat" infusing this play is therefore of a different order from that which draws tears and the common identifications. And it was designed to be of a different order. In a sense, I felt, our situation had thrown us willy-nilly into a new classical period. Classical in the sense that the social scheme, as of old, had reached the point of rigidity where it had become implacable as a consciously known force working in us and upon us. Analytical psychology, when so intensely exploited as to reduce the world to the size of a man's abdomen and equate his fate with his neurosis, is a re-emergence of romanticism. It is inclined to deny all outer forces until man is only his complex. It presupposes an autonomy in the human character that, in a word, is false. A neurosis is not a fate but an effect. There is a higher wisdom, and if truly there is not, there is still no aesthetic point in repeating something so utterly known, or in doing better what has been done so well before.

For me *The Crucible* was a new beginning, the beginning of an attempt to embrace a wider field of vision, a field wide enough to contain the whole of our current awareness. It was not so much to move ahead of the audience but to catch up with what it commonly knows about the way things are and how they get that way. In a word, we commonly know so much more than our plays let on. When we can put together what we do know with what we feel, we shall find a new kind of theatre in our hands. *The Crucible* was written as it was in order to bring me, and the audience, closer to that theatre and what I imagine can be an art more ample than any of us has dared to strive for, the art of Man among men, Man amid his works.

The Crucible: A Structural View

The Crucible is too often spoken of as one of Arthur Miller's less successful plays. Its relative merits as compared with *Death of a Salesman* need not be argued here, but unquestionably the calumny that has been heaped upon it by well-meaning critics is little deserved—the play, however short it may fall of being *the* great American drama, is nevertheless a thoroughly successful, provocative, and stimulating theater piece. When competently performed, it can provide a deeply moving experience for the theatergoer.

The criticism of George Jean Nathan is perhaps typical. Nathan levels four principal charges at the play,[1] charges that in one form or another have been brought against it again and again by other critics. Nathan at least speaks from the advantageous position of having seen the play performed in New York, but too often it appears that wild charges are being flung at the play by critics who have never seen it staged—who have tried, perhaps inexpertly, to capture is full effectiveness from the printed page. This is a hazardous procedure at best, and in the case of *The Crucible* it has led to some gross distortions of what the play says and what it does. Let us examine each of Nathan's four charges and attempt to measure the validity of each.

In the first place, Nathan maintains that the power of the play is all "internal," that it is not communicated to an audience. If we take this criticism to imply that the action occurs within the mind and soul of the protagonist, then of course the statement that the play's power is internal is accurate, but that this in any sense damns the play is belied by the large number of plays throughout dramatic literature that have their action so centered and that are regarded as masterpieces. Most of the plays of Racine can be cited at once in support of this contention, together with selected plays of Euripides, Shakespeare, and Goethe, to name but a few. That *The Crucible* does not communicate this power to an audience is an allegation regarding which empirical evidence is lacking, but the long lines at the box offices of most theaters that have produced it since it "failed" on Broadway constitute, at least in part, a refutation of the charge. At one recent production of which the writer has first-

*By Philip G. Hill. From *Modern Drama,* 10 (Dec., 1967), 312-17. Reprinted by permission.

hand knowledge, all previous attendance records were broken, and experienced theatergoers among the audience testified that they had enjoyed one of the rare and memorable theatrical experiences of their lives. This hardly describes a play that fails to communicate its power to the audience, whatever the quality of the production may have been.

The second charge brought by Nathan against *The Crucible*, and one that is almost universally pressed by those who are dissatisfied with the play, is that it suffers from poor character development. To this charge even the most vehement of its supporters must, in all justice, admit some truth. Elizabeth Proctor is a Puritan housewife, an honest woman, and a bit straight-laced; beyond this we know little of her. John Proctor is an upright and honest farmer confronted by a challenge to his honesty; more can and will be said of the struggles within his soul, but the fact remains that the multifaceted fascination of a Hamlet, an Oedipus, or even of a Willy Loman is indeed lacking. Danforth, on the other hand, is an all-too-recognizable human being: not at all the embodiment of all that is evil, but a conflicting mass of selfish motives and well-intentioned desires to maintain the status quo: not the devil incarnate, but a man convinced that a "good" end (maintaining the theocracy in colonial Massachusetts) can justify the most dubious means—in this case, the suborning of witnesses, the twisting of evidence, and the prostitution of justice. Reverend Hale, too, is a well-developed and many-faceted character, a man who arrives upon the scene confident of his power to exorcise the Devil in whatever form he may appear, and who by the end of the play can challenge every value for which a hero ever died: "Life is God's most precious gift; no principle, however glorious, may justify the taking of it."

Still, it must be admitted that the principal power of *The Crucible* does not lie in its character development. The characters are entirely adequate for the purposes for which Miller designed them, and no immutable law requires that every play depend upon characterization for its success, but certainly there is some justice in suggesting that *The Crucible* exhibits only a moderate degree of character development.

Nathan's next point of criticism is one that was heard from many of the New York critics at the time of the play's original production, but that has ceased to have much potency since the

McCarthy era has passed into history. It was loudly proclaimed in 1953 that *The Crucible* was essentially propagandistic, that it struck too hard at an isolated phenomenon, and that thus it was at best a play of the immediate times and not for all time. The thirteen years that have passed since this charge was leveled, and the continued success of the play both in this country and abroad in the interim, drain from the assertion all of the efficacy that it may once have appeared to have. From the short view inescapably adopted by critics themselves caught up in the hysteria of McCarthyism, the play may well have seemed to push too hard the obvious parallels between witch-hunting in the Salem of 1692 and "witch-hunting" in the Washington and New York of 1952. If so, then we have simply one more reason to be grateful for the passing of this era, for unquestionably the play no longer depends upon such parallels. A whole generation of theater-goers has grown up in these intervening years to whom the name McCarthy is one vaguely remembered from newspaper accounts of the last decade, and who nevertheless find in *The Crucible* a powerful indictment of bigotry, narrow-mindedness, hypocrisy, and violation of due process of law, from whatever source these evils may spring. Unquestionably, if the play were tied inextricably to its alleged connection with a political phenomenon now buried (a connection that Miller denied all along), it would even today not have a very meaningful effect upon its audiences. And yet it does.

The fourth charge against the play, and the one brought by the more serious and insightful of the critics dealing with *The Crucible*, is at the same time the most challenging of the four. For Nathan, together with a host of other critics, attacks the basic structure of the play itself, claiming that it "draws up its big guns" too early in the play, and that by the end of the courtroom scene there is nowhere to go but down. This charge, indeed, gets at the very heart of the matter, and if it can be sustained it largely negates further argument regarding any relative merits that the play might exhibit. I submit, however, that the charge cannot be sustained—that, indeed, the critics adopting such an approach reveal a faulty knowledge of the play's structure and an inaccurate reading of its meaning. Indeed, Miller appears to me to have done a masterful job of sustaining a central action that by its very nature is "internal" and thus not conducive to easy dramatic development, and of sustaining this central action straight through to its logical conclusion at the end of the play.

The term "central action" is being used here in what I take to be its Aristotelian sense: one central objective that provides the play's plot structure with a beginning, a middle, and an end; when the objective is attained, the play is over. This central action may be described in the case of *The Crucible* as "to find John Proctor's soul," where the term "soul" is understood to mean Proctor's integrity, his sense of self-respect, what he himself variously calls his "honesty" and (finally) his "name." Proctor lost his soul, in this sense of the term, when he committed the crime of lechery with Abigail, and thus as the play opens there is wanted only a significant triggering incident to start Proctor actively on the search that will lead ultimately to his death. That this search for Proctor's soul will lead through the vagaries of a witch-hunt, a travesty of justice, and a clear choice between death and life without honor is simply the given circumstance of the play—no more germane to defining its central action than is the fact that Oedipus' search for the killer of Laius will lead through horror and incest to self-immolation. Thinking in these terms, then, it is possible to trace the development of this central action in a straightforward and rather elementary manner.

The structure of the play can conveniently be analyzed in terms of the familiar elements of the well-made play. The initial scenes involving Parris, Abigail, the Putnams, and the other girls serve quite satisfactorily the demands of simple exposition, and pave the way smoothly for the entrance of John Proctor. We learn quickly and yet naturally that a group of girls under Abby's leadership have conjured the Devil and that now at least two of them have experienced hysterical reactions that are being widely interpreted in terms of witchcraft. We also learn, upon Proctor's entrance, of the sexual attraction that still exists between him and Abby, and of the consummation of this attraction that has left John feeling that he has lost his soul. The inciting incident then occurs when Abby assures John that the girls' hysteria has "naught to do with witchcraft," a bit of knowledge that is very shortly to try John's honesty and lead him inevitably to his death.

The rising action of the play continues, then, through the arrival of Hale, Abby's denunciation of certain of the Puritan women (taking her cue from Tituba's success) in order to remove any taint of guilt from herself, and eventually, in the next scene, to the accusation of witchcraft being directed at Elizabeth Proctor. The significant point here, however, is that the rising action continues through the bulk of the courtroom scene, as horror piles upon horror, accusation upon accusation, and complication upon complication, until the action reaches not a climax but a *turning point* when Elizabeth, who purportedly cannot tell a lie, does lie in a misguided attempt to save her husband. This act on her part constitutes a turning point because, from that moment on, Proctor's doom is sealed; no device short of a totally unsatisfactory *deus ex machina* can save him from his inevitable fate. The *central action* of the play is not yet completed, however; Proctor has not yet found his soul, and even moderately skillful playing of the play's final scene can demonstrate quite clearly that this struggle goes on right up to the moment at which Proctor rips up his confession and chooses death rather than dishonor. Thus, this prison scene does not, as some critics have charged, constitute some sort of extended denouement that cannot possibly live up in intensity to the excitement of the courtroom scene, but rather the scene is, in technical terms, the *falling action* of the play, moving inevitably from the turning point to the climax.

This structural significance of the prison scene may be observed in a careful reading of the play, but it is more readily apparent in a competent production. Thus, it is the business of the actor playing Proctor to convey to the audience the fact that signing the confession and then refusing to hand it over to Danforth is not, as has so often been charged, a delaying action and an anticlimactic complication on Miller's part, but rather a continuing and agonizing search on Proctor's part for his honesty—for the course of action that will be truest to his own honor and will recover for him his lost soul. In a dilemma for which there is no simple solution, Proctor first sees the efficacy of Hale's argument, that once life is gone there is no further or higher meaning. Feeling that his honesty has long since been compromised anyway, Proctor seriously feels a greater sense of dishonor in appearing to "go like a saint," as Rebecca and the others do, than in frankly facing up to his own dishonesty and saving his life. On the strength of this argument, he signs the confession. Yet, as Proctor stands there looking at his name on the paper (and here the way in which the actor works with this property becomes all-important), we have a visual, tangible stage metaphor for the struggle that is going on within him. Proctor, unable fully to express the significance of his own plight, cries out:

> Because it is my name! Because I cannot have another in my life! Because I lie and sign myself to lies! Because I am not worth the dust on the feet of them that hang! How may I live without my name? I have given you my soul; leave me my name!

The audience must see that this cry for his "name" is still the same search that has been at the heart of the entire play, and that here it has reached not some kind of anticlimax, but rather *the* climactic moment of the play.

But in stating outright that his confession is a lie (and this is the first moment at which he says so in so many words), Proctor triggers in Danforth the one reaction that seals his own doom. For Danforth, however narrow-minded and bigoted he may be, does indeed believe in the fundamental fact of witchcraft, and he cannot allow a confession that is frankly and openly a lie:

> Is that document a lie? If it is a lie I will not accept it! What say you? I will not deal in lies, Mister! . . . You will give me your honest confession in my hand, or I cannot keep you from the rope. . . . What way do you go, Mister?

Thus stretched to the utmost on the rack of his dilemma, Proctor makes the decision that costs him his life but restores to him his soul: He tears up the confession. The denouement following this climactic moment consumes not a whole scene as has frequently been charged, but a mere twelve lines. Proctor is led out to die, and Elizabeth speaks the epitaph that once again, finally, sums up the central action and significance of the play: "He have his goodness now. God forbid I take it from him!"

Thus, a close structural view of *The Crucible* reveals that this fourth charge against it is also an unfair and inaccurate one. The play, however it may appear in the reading, does not, in performance, rise to a climax in the courtroom scene that cannot be equalled. Certainly the tension of the courtroom scene is great; certainly the prison scene, if poorly performed, could be a letdown. But in a competent performance the inevitable movement from the turning point toward a climax, technically called the "falling action" but certainly involving no falling interest or intensity, continues through the prison scene to that moment at which Proctor rips up his confession, after which a quick denouement brings us to a satisfactory, and at the same time stunning, conclusion.

The play is certainly not one of the great plays of all time. Still, it has been maligned unduly by a series of critics who apparently were either too close to their critical trees to see the theatrical forest or were relying on an inadequate understanding of the play's structure. That this structure is not immediately apparent to the reader, but rather must be brought out in performance, may suggest some degree of weakness in Miller's dramaturgy, but is certainly not a damning weakness in itself. Plays are, after all, written to be performed on a stage, and the ultimate test of their success is their effectiveness under production conditions. *The Crucible* stands up very well to this test.

[1]*The Theatre in the Fifties* (New York: Alfred. A. Knopf Inc., 1953), pp. 105-109.

Appendix I

Historical Documents from the Salem Witchcraft Trials

NOTE: The following excerpts are reprinted from *Records of Salem Witchcraft,* 1864, edited by William E. Woodward. There has been no attempt to change the language of the original documents; punctuation and capitals have been left exactly as they appear in the original documents.

SARAH GOOD

Warrant vs. Sarah Good.
Salem February the 29th 1692
To Constable George Locker.

Whereas Messrs. Joseph Hutchinson, Thomas Putnam, Edward Putnam, and Thomas Preston, Yeomen of Salem Village in the County of Essex, personally appeared before us and made Complaint on Behalf of their Majesties against Sarah Good the wife of William Good of Salem Village abovesaid for suspicion of Witchcraft by her Committed, and thereby much Injury done by Eliz. Parris, Abigail Williams, Ann Putnam and Elizabeth Hubbard all of Salem Village aforesaid Sundry times within this two months and Lately also done, at Salem Village Contrary to the peace of our Sovereign Lord and Lady William & Mary, King & Queen of England etc.—You are therefore in their Majesties' names hereby required to apprehend & bring before us, the said Sarah Good tomorrow about ten of the clock in the forenoon at the house of Lt Nathaniel Ingersoll in Salem Village or as soon as may be then and there to be Examined Relating to the abovesaid premises and hereof you are not to fail at your peril.

Dated. Salem, february 29th 1692

John Hathorne
Jonathan Corwin } Assistants.

Examination of Sarah Good.

The examination of Sarah Good before the worshipful Assistants John Hathorne Jonathan Corwin.

Q. Sarah Good what evil Spirit have you familiarity with
A. None
Q. Have you made no contract with the devil
Good answered no.
Q. Why do you hurt these children
A. I do not hurt them. I scorn it.
Q. Who do you employ then to do it.
A. I employ nobody
Q. What creature do you employ then.
A. no creature but I am falsely accused.
Q. Why did you go away muttering from Mr Parris his house.
A. I did not mutter but I thanked him for what he gave my child.
Q. have you made no contract with the devil.
A. no.

Hathorne desired the children all of them to look upon her and see if this were the person that had hurt them and so they all did look upon her, and said this was one of the persons that did torment them—presently they were all tormented.

Q. Sarah Good do you not see now what you have done, why do you not tell us the truth, why do you thus torment these poor children
A. I do not torment them.
Q. who do you employ then.
A. I employ nobody I scorn it.
Q. how came they thus tormented
A. what do I know you bring others here and now you charge me with it.
Q. why who was it.
A. I do not know but it was some you brought into the meeting house with you.
Q. we brought you into the meeting house.
A. but you brought in two more.
Q. who was it then that tormented the children.
A. it was osborne.
Q. what is it you say when you go muttering away from person's houses

92

A. if I must tell I will tell.

Q. do tell us then

A. if I must tell, I will tell, it is the commandments. I may say my commandments I hope.

Q. what commandment is it.

A. if I must tell I will tell, it is a psalm.

Q. what psalm.

after a long time she muttered over some part of a psalm.

Q. who do you serve

A. I serve God

Q. what God do you serve.

A. the God that made heaven and earth. though she was not willing to mention the word God. her answers were in a very wicked spiteful manner. reflecting and retorting against the authority with base and abusive words and many lies she was taken in it was here said that her husband had said that he was afraid that she either was a witch or would be one very quickly. the worshipful Mr. Hawthorne asked him his reason why he said so of her, whether he had ever seen anything of her, he answered no, not in this nature, but it was her bad carriage to him, and indeed said he I may say with tears that she is an enemy to all good.

Salem Village March the 1st 1692

Written by Ezekiel Cheever . . .

Dated Salem March 29th 1692

Sarah Good upon Examination denieth the matter of fact (viz) that she ever used any witchcraft or hurt the abovesaid children or any of them.

The above-named Children being all present positively accused her of hurting of them Sundry times within this two months and also that morning.

Sarah Good being Asked if, that she did not then hurt them who did it. And the children being again tortured she looked upon them And said that it was one of them we brought into the house with us. We asked her who it was, she then Answered and said it was Sarah Osborne, and Sarah Osborne was then under Custody and not in the house; And the children being quickly after recovered out of their fit said that it was Sarah Good and also Sarah Osborne that then did hurt & torment or afflict them—although both of them at the same time at a distance or Remote from them personally—there were also sundry other Questions put to her and Answers given thereunto by her according as is also given in.

John Hathorne
Jonathan Corwin } Assistants

The Examination of Tituba.

Q. Tituba what evil spirit have you familiarity with.

A. none.

Q. why do you hurt these children.

A. I do not hurt them.

Q. who is it then.

A. the devil for aught I know.

Q. Did you never see the devil.

A. The devil came to me and bid me serve him.

Q. Who have you seen.

A. Four women sometimes hurt the children.

Q. Who were they.

A. Goody Osborne and Sarah Good and I do not know who the other were. Sarah Good and Osborne would have me hurt the children but I would not she further saith there was a tall man of Boston that she did see.

Q. when did you see them.

A. Last night at Boston.

Q. what did they say to you.

A. they said hurt the children

Q. and did you hurt them

A. no there is 4 women and one man they hurt the children and they lay all upon me and they tell me if I will not hurt the children they will hurt me.

Q. but did you not hurt them

A. yes, but I will hurt them no more.

Q. are you not sorry you did hurt them.

A. yes.

Q. and why then do you hurt them.

A. they say hurt children or we will do worse to you.

Q. what have you seen.

A. an man come to me and say serve me.

Q. what service.

A. hurt the children and last night there was an appearance that said kill the children and if I would no[t] go on hurting the children they would do worse to me.

Q. what is this appearance you see.

A. Sometimes it is like a hog and sometimes like a great dog, this appearance she saith she did see 4 times.

Q. what did it say to you

A. it . . . the black dog said serve me but I said I am afraid he said if I did not he would do worse to me.

Q. what did you say to it.

A. I will serve you no longer. then he said he would hurt me and then he looked like a man and threatens to hurt me, she said that this man had a yellow bird that kept with him and he told me he had more pretty things that he would give me if I would serve him.

Q. what were these pretty things.

A. he did not show me them.

Q. what also have you seen

A. two rats, a red rat and a black rat.

Q. what did they say to you.

A. they said serve me.

Q. when did you see them.

A. last night and they said serve me, but I said I would not

Q. what service.

A. she said hurt the children.

Q. did you not pinch Elizabeth Hubbard this morning

A. the man brought her to me and made me pinch her

Q. why did you go to Thomas Putnam's last night and hurt his child.

A. they pull and haul me and make me go

Q. and what would have you do.

A. Kill her with a knife.

Lieutenant Fuller and others said at this time when the child saw these persons and was tormented by them that she did complain of a knife, that they would have her cut her head off with a knife.

Q. how did you go

A. we ride upon sticks and are there presently.

Q. why did you not tell your master.

A. I was afraid they said they would cut off my head if I told.

Q. would you not have hurt others if you could.

A. They said they would hurt others but they could not

Q. what attendants hath Sarah Good.

A. a yellow bird and she would have given me one

Q. what meat did she give it

A. it did suck her between her fingers

Q. did not you hurt Mr Currin's child

A. goody good and goody Osborne told that they did hurt Mr Currin's child and would have had me hurt him too, but I did not.

Q. what hath Sarah Osborne.

A. yellow dog, she had a thing with a head like a woman with 2 legs, and wings. Abigail Williams that lives with her Uncle Parris said that she did see the same creature, and it turned into the shape of Goody Osborne.

Q. what else have you seen with Osborne.

A. another thing, hairy it goes upright like a man it hath only 2 legs.

Q. did you not see Sarah Good upon Elizabeth Hubbard, last Saturday.

A. I did see her set a wolf upon her to afflict her, the persons with this maid did say that she did complain of a wolf. . . . she further saith that she saw a cat with good at another time.

Q. What clothes doth the man go in

A. he goes in black clothes a tall man with white hair I think

Q. How doth the woman go

A. in a white hood and a black hood with a top knot

Q. do you see who it is that torments these children now.

A. yes it is Goody Good, she hurts them in her own shape

Q. and who is it that hurts them now.

A. I am blind now. I cannot see.

Salem Village
March the 1st 1692

Written by Ezekiel Cheever
Salem Village March 1st 1692

96

JOHN PROCTOR

Mary Warren's Examination

Q. Whether you did not know that it was the Devil's book when you signed.

A. I did not know it then but I know it now to be sure it was the Devil's book, in the first place to be sure I did set my hand to the devil's book: I have considered of it since you were here last and it was the devil's book that my Master Proctor brought to me and he told me if I would set my hand to that book I should believe and I did set my hand to it but...it was done with my finger. he brought the book and told me if I would take the book and touch it that I should be well and I thought then that it was the Devil's book.

Q. Was there not your consent to hurt the children when you were hurt? and said if you are afflicted I wish they were more afflicted and you and all: I said Master what makes you say so. He answered, because you go to bring out Innocent persons, I told him that that could not be. and whether the Devil took advantage at that I know not to afflict them and one night talking about them I said I did not care though they were tormented if ye charged me.

Q. Did you ever see any puppets?

A. Yes once I saw one made of cloth in Mistress Proctor's hand.

Q. Who was it like, or which of the Children was it for?

A. I cannot tell, whether for Ann Putnam or Abigail Williams for one of them it was I am sure, it was in my mistress's hand.

Q. What did you stick into the puppet?

A. I did stick in a pin about the neck of it as it was in Proctor's hand.

Q. How many more did you see afterwards?

A. I do not remember that ever I saw any more.

Mary Warren v. John Proctor

The deposition of Mary Warren aged 20 years he[re] testifieth. I have seen the apparition of John Proctor senior among the witches and he hath often tortured me by pinching me and biting me and choking me, and pressing me on my Stomach till the blood came out of my mouth and also I saw him torture

Mis Pope and Mercy lewis and John Indian upon the day of his examination and he hath also tempted me to write in his book. and to eat bread which he brought to me, which I refusing to do, Jno Proctor did most grievously torture me with variety of tortures, almost Ready to kill me.

Mary Warren owned the above written upon her oath before and unto the Grand Inquest on the 30 Day of June 1692

Selected Criticisms

Arthur Miller is a problem playwright, in both senses of the word. As a man of independent thought, he is profoundly, angrily concerned with the immediate issues of our society—with the irresponsible pressures which are being brought to bear on free men, with the self-seeking which blinds whole segments of our civilization to justice, with the evasions and dishonesties into which cowardly men are daily slipping. And to his fiery editorializing he brings shrewd theatrical gifts: He knows how to make a point plain, how to give it bite in the illustration, how to make its caustic and cauterizing language ring out on the stage.

He is also an artist groping toward something more poetic than simple, savage journalism. He has not only the professional crusader's zeal for humanity, but the imaginative writer's feeling for it—how it really behaves, how it moves about a room, how it looks in its foolish as well as in its noble attitudes—and in his best play, *Death of a Salesman*, he was able to rise above the sermon and touch the spirit of some simple people.

In *The Crucible*, which opened at the Martin Beck Thursday, he seems to me to be taking a step backward into mechanical parable, into the sort of play which lives not in the warmth of humbly observed human souls but in the ideological heat of polemic.

Make no mistake about it: There is fire in what Mr. Miller has to say, and there is a good bit of sting in his manner of saying it. He has, for convenience's sake, set his troubling narrative in the Salem of 1692. For reasons of their own, a quartet of exhibitionistic young women are hurling accusations of witchcraft at eminently respectable members of a well-meaning, but not entirely clear-headed, society.

On the basis of hearsay—"guilt by association with the devil" might be the phrase for it—a whole community of innocents are brought to trial and condemned to be hanged. As Mr. Miller pursues his very clear contemporary parallel, there are all sorts of relevant thrusts: The folk who do the final damage are not the lunatic fringe but the gullible pillars of society; the courts bog down into travesty in order to comply with the popular mood; slander becomes the weapon of opportunists ("Is the accuser always holy now?"); freedom is possible at the price of naming one's associates in crime; even the upright man is eventually tormented into going along with the mob to secure his own way of life, his own family.

Much of this—not all—is an accurate reading of our own turbulent age, and there are many times at the Martin Beck when one's intellectual sympathies go out to Mr. Miller and to his apt symbols anguishing on the stage. But it is the intellect which goes out, not the heart. . . .

By Walter Kerr. From the *New York Herald Tribune*, Jan. 23, 1953, p. 12.

Arthur Miller has written another powerful play. *The Crucible*, it is called, and it opened at the Martin Beck last evening in an equally powerful performance. Riffling back the pages of American history, he has written the drama of the witch trials and hangings in Salem in 1692. Neither Mr. Miller nor his audiences are unaware of certain similarities between the perversions of justice then and today.

But Mr. Miller is not pleading a cause in dramatic form. For *The Crucible*, despite its current implications, is a self-contained play about a terrible period in American history. Silly accusations of witchcraft by some mischievous girls in Puritan dress gradually take possession of Salem. Before the play is over, good people of pious nature and responsible temper are condemning other good people to the gallows.

Having a sure instinct for dramatic form, Mr. Miller goes bluntly to essential situations. John Proctor and his wife, farm people, are the central characters of the play. At first the idea that Goodie Proctor is a witch is only an absurd rumor. But *The Crucible* carries the Proctors through the whole ordeal—first vague suspicion, then the arrest, the implacable, highly wrought trial in the church vestry, the final opportunity for John Proctor to save his neck by confessing to something he knows is a lie, and finally the baleful roll of the drums at the foot of the gallows.

Although *The Crucible* is a powerful drama, it stands second to *Death of a Salesman* as a work of art. Mr. Miller has had more trouble with this one, perhaps because he is too conscious of its implications. The literary style is cruder. The early motivation is muffled in the uproar of the opening scene, and the theme does not develop with the simple eloquence of *Death of a Salesman.*

It may be that Mr. Miller has tried to pack too much inside his drama, and that he has permitted himself to be concerned more with the technique of the witch hunt than with its humanity. For all its power generated on the surface, *The Crucible* is most moving in the simple, quiet scenes between John Proctor and his wife. By the standards of *Death of a Salesman*, there is too much excitement and not enough emotion in *The Crucible*. . . .

After the experience of *Death of a Salesman* we probably expect Mr. Miller to write a masterpiece every time. *The Crucible* is not of that stature and it lacks that universality. On a lower level of dramatic history with considerable pertinence for today, it is a powerful play and a genuine contribution to the season.

By Brooks Atkinson. From The New York Times, Jan. 23, 1953, p.15.

The issue of civil liberty is too serious to be confused by its defenders as well as its enemies. Freedom is under menacing fire at home as well as abroad. But Arthur Miller, in his new play *The Crucible*, seems to us to have provided more confusion than defense.

Some may argue—as many of the drama critics did—that this is just a play about Salem, Mass., in the time of the 1692 witch hunt. Having seen it ourselves, we dissent. It is inconceivable that Miller is unaware that the year is 1953 and that a play about Salem's witch hunt was inevitably bound to stir contemporary echoes.

The trouble is that the inferences are deceptive and, in an important sense, invalid. Whatever his original intention, Miller has pushed the people of Salem around in a loaded allegory which may shed some light on their time but ultimately succeeds in muddying our own.

The frenzied cruelty of Salem stemmed from superstition and fantasy: Lives were ruined and lost in the wild attempt to prove that witches were the root of all suffering. In Miller's script the labored implication is that modern political hysteria is similarly founded on totally irrational fear of nonexistent demons.

It would be nice if life were that simple. . . .

From the New York Post, February 1, 1953, p.9M.

There has been some debate as to whether this story of seventeenth-century Salem "really" refers to our current "witch hunt" yet since no one is interested in anything *but* this reference, I pass on to the real point at issue, which is: the validity of the parallel. It is true in that people today are being persecuted on quite chimerical grounds. It is untrue in that communism is not, to put it mildly, merely a chimera. The word communism is used to cover, first, the politics of Marx, second, the politics of the Soviet Union, and, third, the activities of all liberals as they seem to illiberal illiterates. Since Mr. Miller's argument bears only on the third use of the word, its scope is limited. Indeed, the analogy between "red-baiting" and witch hunting can seem complete only to communists, for only to them is the menace of communism as fictitious as the menace of witches. The non-communist will look for certain reservations and provisos. In *The Crucible*, there are none.

To accuse Mr. Miller of communism would of course be to fall into the trap of oversimplification which he himself has set. For all I know he may hate the Soviet state with all the ardor of Eisenhower. What I am maintaining is that his view of life is dictated by assumptions which liberals have to unlearn and which many liberals have rather publicly unlearned. Chief among these assumptions is that of general innocence. In Hebrew mythology, innocence was lost at the very beginning of things; in liberal, especially American liberal, folklore, it has not been lost yet; Arthur Miller is the playwright of American liberal folklore. It is as if the merely negative, and legal, definition of innocence were extended to the rest of life: you are innocent until proved guilty, you are innocent if you "didn't do it." Writers have a sort of double innocence: not only can they create innocent characters, they can also write from the viewpoint of innocence—we can speak today not only of the "omniscient" author but of the "guiltless" one. . . .

By Eric Bentley. From *What Is Theatre? Incorporating "The Dramatic Event" and Other Reviews 1944-1967* (New York: Atheneum, 1968), pp. 62-65.

Despite the fact that he is often at his best in the "realist" vein, Mr. Miller, like any good heir of the thirties, is preoccupied with ideology. He has a richer personal sense of it than comparable writers, but the impulse remains unaltered. His characteristic theme is integrity, and its obverse, compromise. In earlier plays, Miller frequently brought to this subject a distressing note of stridency; one often felt that, really, the battle had long since been won, and that this continued obsession with it was an indication not of seriousness, but perhaps of some arrested moral development.

In *The Crucible*, however, he has stated his theme again with a wholly admirable concision and force. His central figure is John Proctor, another spokesman for rational feeling and the disinterested intelligence. Proctor is so patently the enemy of hysteria that his very existence is a challenge to the fanatic temperament, and he is consumed by its malice. What gives the situation a fresh vitality is Miller's really painful grasp of its ambiguities: the dilemma of a man, fallible, subject to pride, but forced to choose between the "negative good" of truth and morality, and the "positive good" of human life under any dispensation. Around this crisis of conscience, Mr. Miller has written an exhaustive, exacerbated scene—one of his most truly distinguished, and one which most hopefully displays the expanding delicacy of his moral imagination.

It is difficult, however, to feel that the political complexities inherent in *The Crucible* have been approached by Mr. Miller with any comparable sensitivity. He has, admittedly, disclaimed intent of contemporary reference in the play, choosing to see in it only the tragedy of another society. But it would be fatuous of Mr. Miller to pretend that our present cultural climate had not always a place in the foreground of his mind. Surely then, he can see that the Salem witch-hunts and our own virulent varieties are parallel only in their effects, not in their causes. . . .

By Richard Hayes. From *Commonweal* 57, Feb. 1953, p. 498.

Suggested Study Topics

1. Look up the word "crucible" in a dictionary. In an essay, discuss the reasons that may have led Miller to select the word for his play's title.

2. Write an essay on one or more of the following: theme, setting, structure, language and plot.

3. Discuss and compare Deputy Governor Danforth, Reverend Hale and John Proctor.

4. In *After the Fall*, Miller covered some of the same material that prompted him to write *The Crucible*. Since some critics feel that Miller should not have ventured into the difficult realm of historical drama, a comparison of the two plays may be helpful. Write an essay on which is the more successful play for Miller.

5. Aristotle, in his *Poetics*, defined tragedy as dealing with human suffering and human courage (to be tragic, doom must be resisted, not accepted passively) capable of leaving the audience emotionally purged and exalted. Is *The Crucible* a tragedy in the Aristotelian sense? Is John Proctor a tragic hero in the Aristotelian sense — one who may suffer from a defect of character, but who recognizes his fate and accepts it knowingly?

6. A frequent criticism of *The Crucible* is that its characters are more symbolic than real. Do you agree or disagree? Why?

7. Do you think that the parallel between Salem's 17th century witch hunt and the "witch hunt" of the McCarthy era in the United States is valid? Explain the use of the word "witch hunt" as it applied to the 1950s.

8. Compare the characterizations of Susanna, Mercy, Betty, Mary and Abigail. Are they credible young people? What makes them behave as they do? Do you think their modern equivalents could produce a similar wave of terror? Discuss these ideas in an essay.

9. Various playwrights — notably Ibsen, Strindberg, O'Neill and Odets — are believed to have influenced Miller. Choose one of these authors and compare his work with Miller's, especially *The Crucible*.

Bibliography

Adler, Henry, "To Hell With Society," *Tulane Drama Review*, IV, 4 (May, 1960).

Bentley, Eric. *The Dramatic Event*. Boston, 1954.

Bergeron, David M. "Arthur Miller's *The Crucible* and Nathaniel Hawthorne: Some Parallels." *English Journal*, 58 (January 1969), pp. 47-55.

Bermel, Albert. "Right, Wrong and Mr. Miller," *The New York Times*, April 14, 1968, II, pp. 1 and 7.

Bettina, Sister M., SSND, "Willy Loman's Brother Ben: Tragic Insight in *Death of a Salesman*," *Modern Drama*, IV (February, 1962).

Clurman, Harold. "Arthur Miller: Theme and Variations," *Theatre, The Annual of the Repertory Theater of Lincoln Center*, ed. Barry Hyams. New York, 1964.

Clurman, Harold. *Lies Like Truth*. New York, 1958.

Corrigan, Robert W. *Arthur Miller: A Collection of Critical Essays*, Englewood Cliffs, 1969.

Dillingham, William B. "Arthur Miller and the Loss of Consciousness," *Emory University Quarterly*, XVI (Spring, 1960), pp. 40-50.

Eissenstat, Martha Turnquist. "Arthur Miller: A Bibliography," *Modern Drama*, V (May, 1962).

Ferres, John H. *Twentieth Century Interpretations of the Crucible*. Englewood Cliffs, 1972.

Findlater, Richard. "No Time for Tragedy?" *Twentieth Century,* CLXI (January, 1957).

Ganz, Arthur. "The Silence of Arthur Miller," *Drama Survey*, III, ii (October, 1963).

_____. "Arthur Miller: After the Silence," *Drama Survey,* III (1964).

Gardner, R. H. *The Splintered Stage*. New York, 1965.

Gould, Jean. *Modern American Playwrights*. New York, 1966.

Hayashi, Tetsumaro. *An Index to Arthur Miller Criticism*. Metuchen, N.J., 1976.

Hayes, Richard. "I Want My Catharsis," *Commonweal*, LXIII (November 4, 1955).

Hogan, Robert. *Arthur Miller*. Minneapolis: University of Minnesota Press, 1964.

Huftel, Sheila. *Arthur Miller: The Burning Glass*, New York, 1965.

Hunt, Albert. "Realism and Intelligence: Some Notes on Arthur Miller," *Encore*, VII, London (May-June, 1960).

Lerner, Max. *Actions and Passions*. New York, 1949.

McAnany, Emile G., S.J. "The Tragic Commitment: Some Notes on Arthur Miller," *Modern Drama*, V (1962).

Moss, Leonard. "Arthur Miller and the Common Man's Language," *Modern Drama*, VII (1964).

Newnan, William J. "Arthur Miller's Collected Plays," *Twentieth Century*, CLXIV (Nov., 1958).

Popkin, Henry. "Arthur Miller: The Strange Encounter," *Sewanee Review*, LXVIII (Winter, 1960).

Rahv, Phillip. *The Myth and the Powerhouse*. New York, 1965.

Schneider, Daniel E., M.D. "A Study of Two Plays by Arthur Miller," *The Psychoanalyst and the Artist* by Daniel E. Schneider, M.D. New York, 1950.

Seagar, Allan. "The Creative Agony of Arthur Miller," *Esquire*, LII (October, 1959).

Tynan, Kenneth. *Curtains*. New York, 1961.

Walker, Philip. "Arthur Miller's *The Crucible*: Tragedy or Allegory?" *Western Speech* 20 (Fall, 1956), pp. 222-24.

Weales, Gerald. *American Drama Since World War II*. New York, 1962.

Death of a Salesman, Text and Criticism, The Viking Critical Library edition. New York, 1967.

Welland, Dennis. *Arthur Miller*. New York, 1961.

Wiegand, William. "Arthur Miller and the Man Who Knows," *Western Review*, XXI (1957).